Dedication

This book is dedicated to my parents. Thank you for all your love and support. Without you, none of this would be possible. I love you!

IMPERATIVE

How any business can quickly and easily
leverage mobile marketing for radical success

Brett Relander

The information presented herein represents the views of the author as of the date of publication. This book is presented for informational purposes only. Due to the rate at which conditions change, the author reserves the right to alter and update his opinions at any time. While every attempt has been made to verify the information in this book, the author does not assume any responsibility for errors, inaccuracies, or omissions.

Library of Congress Control Number: 2014909173
CreateSpace Independent Publishing Platform
North Charleston, South Carolina

Contents

IMPERATIVE

□ □ □

If you don't like change, you're going
to like irrelevance even less.

– **General Eric Shinseky** (ret.),
United States Secretary of Veterans Affairs

Introduction

I don't have to tell you that mobile devices have changed the way we live.

Have you ever left home without your mobile phone? Chances are, you hurried back for it. Most people would rather be without their wallet than their mobile phone. And who can blame us? If you're like me, your whole life is organized on that little machine. You use it for your calendar and to check email. It's likely you keep your contacts list on your phone. How many phone numbers do you know by heart anymore? We use our mobiles to update our social media status, read headlines, and check weather and sports scores. We keep up with trends in our industries and we send a quick text when we're running late or to confirm the address of our next meeting. We take and send pictures from our mobile devices and even check our bank balances and pay bills. We customize our mobile devices with apps and features that entertain us, entertain our kids, simplify and enhance our lives.

Sure, we choose to disconnect on occasion. We turn off our ringers when we enjoy dinner with the people we care about or when we go to a movie. But that's the exception; the majority of the time, our phones are both activated and within easy reach.

It's hard to remember what it was like when we had a pile of paper maps folded in the glove boxes of our cars and when we had to stop at a pay phone to communicate a change of plans. There must have been a time when we stayed at the office later waiting for that last email or (remember?) fax and couldn't just check our phones from the sidelines of our kids' soccer games.

We're untethered. We have become accustomed to the freedom of being able to access information at any time and from any place. In order to connect with work, friends, and our favorite brands, we're no longer tied to our offices and homes. We can be anywhere and still do the things we need (and want) to do. That instantaneous and limitless access has become so integrated into our habits that it's changing the way we live, think, work, and play.

And, from a business perspective, it's certainly changing the way we reach out to customers.

Just as our mobile phones and tablets have become an indispensable part of the way we run our daily lives, mobile marketing has morphed into an essential aspect of basic business practice.

Mobile customers are on the move and are accustomed to controlling the information they receive and the timing with which they receive it. Not so long ago, marketers could only deliver their message by creating commercials and running them during the breaks of their customers' favorite TV shows, or by placing advertisements in magazines or on the radio. That was back in the day when people sat still, were engaged with one form of media at a time, and were captive listeners.

That was before mobile – an era our kids regard as existing somewhere between cave dwelling and steam trains.

When was the last time you sat on your sofa and watched an entire television program, commercials and all? Customers control their media choices. Print magazines and newspapers are giving way to digital counterparts, and consumers can control the messages and information that comes into their homes. And let's not even get started on the irritating and environmentally irresponsible mountains of junk mail that are printed, trucked, shoved into mailboxes, and promptly discarded.

Mobile is as close as a customer's pocket, it's highly individual, customizable, and it's always on.

□ □ □

Television and movie screens offer essentially passive entertainment. The customer sits back and programming is delivered. You watch or you don't. Computer screens offer more interactive options. With the personal computer, customers are sociable, interactive, and are able to customize and search for the products and programming that appeals to them. Mobile takes it a step further. With mobile, customers can communicate directly and instantly from anyplace in the world, taking the screens out of the living rooms and offices and into the real world playground.

To be competitive, brands have no choice but to make mobile marketing a key component of their overall marketing plans. Your customers expect to access information about your products and services from their mobile devices. At minimum, your site must be mobile optimized, quick, informative, and easy to use.

This is a book for anyone who wants to grow his or her brand. It's for anyone with a business of any size who wants to connect with their customers. This is a book for anyone who is serious about providing optimal customer service and an amazing customer experience. It's a book for people who are ready to think about their brand, to get into the minds of their customers, and to ask how they can serve them better.

You've chosen this book because you want to learn more about the possibilities of a mobile campaign and the step-by-step recipes to implementing tactics that reach your customers where they are and deliver meaningful and timely content. I have to warn you, though – this isn't the kind of book that you sit down and read and then put back on the shelf. Whether you're reading a print version or (more likely) are accessing these words from a mobile device, there are plenty of opportunities for interaction. I want you to use this book as a springboard for action. And so I'm going to ask you to explore a little. I'll give you the groundwork and then ask the questions that you need to get started on a mobile campaign immediately. In addition, I'm including interactive features that will help to illustrate the options and opportunities inherent in mobile media. And, at the end of each tactical section, there will be a simple set up guide or checklist that you can follow to include mobile in your marketing mix now.

In this book, we'll explore how to create relevant content for mobile that is accessible, actionable and authentic. We'll look at the history of mobile, get a clear picture of what is happening in mobile now, and will establish ways to break ground in the future. Remembering that mobile is a great medium for innovation, we'll learn to test and adapt a campaign in order to learn from the input and habits of your customers so that you can best serve them and grow your brand.

I'll tell you a little bit about the staggering facts and the stats relating to mobile devices and the growing number of people across the world who are using mobile daily for every imaginable activity and convenience.

Over the course of this book, I'll give you real-world context of how mobile is reshaping the way we think and act, and how these changes in society will influence the ways you reach out to your customers. I'll also explain how to create a mobile strategy that works, is relevant, and serves both your customers and your goals.

Mobile marketing is exciting and involves a little bit of risk-taking. But in today's competitive marketplace, it's not optional. I don't know about you, but I'm not willing to lose the customers who want to connect with me and my company with their mobile devices.

We'll explore the rules of mobile and investigate the evolving etiquette of interacting on mobile devices. We'll work through and customize strategies for creating a mobile campaign and explore options of how to implement, test, and adapt that campaign for optimal results. In order to optimize your customer relationships using mobile marketing, I'll teach you to identify opportunities by asking the right questions with the goal of connecting with your customers.

To wrap it all up, I'll reveal step-by-step tactics you can use to implement your strategy, and will teach you how to test and refine your program to measure and achieve optimal results.

Remember, this isn't the kind of book you passively read. In each of the tactical sections, I've included an interactive feature so that in addition to reading how to put the tactics to work for your brand, you'll be able to experience first hand, and instantly, the ways these tactics inspire interaction and engagement.

INTRODUCTION

□ □ □

I want to hear from you. As you use this book I invite you to let me know what's working for you and what I can do to better serve you. You can find me at LaunchandHustle.com. We've created a membership community where you can share your success and learn from others who are using mobile marketing and social media in creative ways. I'd love to hear how you're using mobile to serve your customers, and I'm happy to answer questions and to continue to brainstorm better ways to engage customers and reach them where they are. This book is a solid starting point, and I believe it will give you the tools you need to launch a mobile campaign. But as a medium, mobile is evolving quickly, and I want to offer you the resources to stay current and continue the conversation.

Let's stay in touch.

And now we begin!

□ □ □

Going Mobile

□ □ □

1. The Staggering Facts

You already know that our reliance on mobile devices is shaping our culture. I want to share with you some numbers that will illustrate the scale of this revolution as well as the speed and scope of the evolution of mobile.

According to *eMarketer, smartphone users worldwide will total 1.75 billion in 2014 with 4.55 billion people worldwide to use a mobile phone.* Hardware turnover is fast and steady as cell phone service providers often offer free or steeply discounted upgrade plans every two years. You can almost count on most mobile devices being replaced every other year. Between 2013 and 2017, mobile phone penetration is expected to rise from 61.1% to 69.4% of the global population, according to eMarketer.

According to comScore, 159.8 million people in the U.S. owned smartphones (66.8 percent mobile market penetration) during the three months ending in January 2014, up 7 percent since October and 24% since 2012.

Smartphone users aren't just kids; in 2011, smartphone usage increased by 92% among retirees (*comScore 2012*) and the tablet market shows great promise for aging Americans as well.

Texting is one of the simplest and most beloved features on mobile devices. In a survey of mothers of young children, they stated that the text message feature was the single most important feature on their mobile devices and ranked it above the ability to make calls. Americans send and receive over 6 billion text messages every day. A quick two-way form of communication, the text message is designed to discreetly and efficiently get the attention of the recipient. We text to let each other know when we'll be late for dinner. We check in with our kids. We donate money to charity. We share a quick joke and using multimedia-messaging service (MMS), people send instant photos, links, and even movies to friends and relatives.

Smartphone users love apps. Mobile analytics firm Flurry measured overall time spent on U.S. iOS and Android devices and found that app usage now takes up 86% of time spent on mobile. That's up from an 80% in 2013. The growing app usage trend comes at the expense of the mobile web, which now makes up just 14% of time spent on mobile devices.

> **app usage now takes up 86% of time spent on mobile.**

We use apps for everything from playing games to checking bank balances. We check the weather, follow our favorite sports teams, read the day's headlines, entertain our kids, organize our time, set goals, connect with social media outlets, share photos and ideas, keep track of our exercise, check prices, and research buying decisions. It's no wonder we don't leave home without our mobile devices. We manage our lives with these little machines.

We like to browse. According to StatCounter mobile now drives about 22% of global internet traffic and nearly 19% in the US. That doesn't include the internet activity that originates from apps, social media, or other direct links – that's just people searching for specific things with a browser from their mobile device.

If the analytics on your existing site are typical, 30-40% of your customers are likely accessing your site from a mobile device. Are you ready for them?

We expect sites to be mobile-friendly. It's frustrating trying to navigate a site with tiny fonts, broad margins and slow-to-load features. Sixty-one percent of people who visit a site that isn't optimized for mobile will move on to a competitor's site (*Karim Temsamani at IABALM 2012 via IAB*). Mobile users tend to be focused on their task, and if they can't quickly and easily access the information they desire on their first try, they'll go on to the next option. The good news is, they are also motivated, and mobile users are more likely to act on calls to action than desktop users are, and they do so usually within minutes. For instance, according to xAd and Telemetrics, mobile searches related to restaurants have a conversion rate of 90% with 64% converting within the hour. First impressions, in mobile, are huge.

According to Google, 84% of smartphone shoppers use their devices to help shop while in the store. People are serious about comparison-shopping with their mobile devices in hand; one in five smartphone users have scanned product barcodes. In December 2011, Amazon drew media attention to this practice when they offered a five percent credit to customers who downloaded and used their price checker app to scan an item in a brick and mortar store that they would ultimately purchase on Amazon. This promotion spawned significant debate as people expressed concern that Amazon was anti-small business. Meanwhile, price-conscious customers responded by downloading the app and claimed the discount during the busy holiday season. The analogy persists of brick and mortar businesses serving as showrooms for online retailers, and many small businesses are responding by focusing on creating positive experiences for customers in-store in conjunction with offering multi-channel digital convenience.

In 2011, quick response (QR) code scans increased by a whopping 300% (*ScanLife*). QR codes are showing up everywhere from in-store signs to stickers on bananas, and customers are becoming increasingly comfortable scanning them. QR codes give the marketer a chance to inform and entertain the curious customer. A customer can order coffee and pay for it using QR codes or can shop for household items. Retailers such as Macy's have integrated QR codes into media-rich campaigns offering their customers additional behind the scenes content and discounts to enhance the traditional shopping experience. QR codes are also becoming ubiquitous in print ads. In the top 100 magazines in the US, QR code usage grew by 617% (*Nellymoser*).

IMPERATIVE

Checking email is the single most popular activity on a smartphone. As more people access their email from mobile devices, they're using their desktops less frequently for email. In December 2013 the email open rate from mobile devices grew to 51%, and desktop open rates dropped to 24% (*Litmus* –"Email Analytics" Jan 2014). As we become more mobile, we're doing more activities from mobile devices that once had to occur at a desk. We've had a clear shift in expectations whereby we used to expect someone to respond to an email within a day, and now we start wondering what happened if they don't get back to us within an hour. And with text messages, we expect a response within minutes.

Have you looked up the address of a coffee shop or the hours of a local retail outlet? Sixty-one percent of smartphone users have conducted a local search within fifteen miles of their current location (*Localeze/15miles Fifth Annual comScore Local Search Usage Study February 2012*). Over half of all local searches are performed on a mobile device (*Google*); in addition, 49% have used apps to search for local businesses.

We're impulsive and are getting used to having information as close as our pocket. 40% of all restaurant searches are mobile. 35% of movie searches are made with a mobile device (*Google*). And over a third of the people surveyed said that they would buy a movie ticket from their mobile device.

Mobile coupons are more likely to be redeemed than paper coupons. Some mobile coupons are available by applications and others are sent in mobile email, through websites, or as a promo code via SMS.

There are many ways to make payments with mobile devices and more are emerging. Payments are expected to quadruple in 2014 to $630 billion dollars (*Juniper Research*).

U.S. mobile travel bookings will more than triple from 2012 to 2014, when mobile bookings will reach US$25.8 billion. (*PhoCusWright, February 2013*).

As you can tell, regardless of your industry or your companies size, mobile marketing and a clear strategy are essential to your success.

□ □ □

2. The Shortfalls of Traditional Marketing

Traditional marketing channels are becoming obsolete. Both as someone trying to promote your brand as well as by your own experience as a consumer, I'm sure you've learned many of the pitfalls of traditional marketing.

Just the other day, I was visiting a friend at his condo. On the table was a pile of mail full of glossy flyers sent from an independent energy company, landscape company, lawyers, dentists, realtors, etc. How much money had they spent creating and mailing this advertising that the intended recipients would likely never see? I went home and realized that I had received the same flyers in my own mail. I dropped it immediately into the recycle bin and couldn't help reflecting on the sheer wastefulness of the campaign. Not only was the campaign likely fail as it wasn't targeted, it had to have been costly – the price of the bulk postage alone must have been staggering. And I don't even want to think about what this kind of waste does to the environment.

Yes, there are many shortfalls of traditional marketing. Television commercials, print ads, and sponsored outdoor advertising rely on projecting out to a passive and (hopefully) receptive crowd. It's inexact at best. At worst, it's expensive, difficult to track and irritating to the same crowd you're trying to attract. While waiting for the subway, you might see an advertisement that interests you. But, how long will you remember it? And what are the chances you'll actually take the next step and seek out that particular brand of jeans, sneakers, beer or air-conditioning repair service? Not very likely. In traditional advertising, marketers expect the customer to seek out the brand organically, after only an impression or two. They rely upon the memory of consumers and expect that they will take action at some future unspecified date. Advertisers and marketers attempt to persuade customers to associate positively with a brand by creating aspirational content and hope that it resonates and is remembered. In fact, an axiom of traditional advertising is that the consumer must see the message repeatedly before they're expected to remember it.

It's a wait and see approach. And it only works some of the time. It's not relevant to the fast-paced way we tend to live today and the way the new age customer consumes content.

The world is changing. We're bombarded by messages all day every day. We have been forced to become selective. Just because we receive a flyer in the mail doesn't mean we will take the time to read it.

With all the chatter we encounter every day, how likely are we to remember the brand of jeans we saw advertised on our morning commute? How likely are we to remember that we needed new jeans at all? And when we do decide we need or want new jeans, what will likely influence our purchasing decision?

Individuals have become authorities. We no longer turn to experts to tell us what to buy. And we certainly don't appreciate advertisers suggesting how we should live our lives. We've grown used to having access to unlimited and instant information. We take for granted our ability to compare products and services at a moment's notice and get exactly what we want when we need it.

We're reassured by our ability to research and we're not afraid to experiment and to go outside of our expertise. When we want to know how to make the best margarita, we Google a recipe. If one forgets how to tie a Windsor knot, there are dozens of instructional videos on YouTube. We can quickly and easily find and follow step-by-step instructions to repair home electronics, install new bookshelves, write a resume, and throw a party. We have become content creators and curators as we post our activities on social networks. We are pundits and bloggers. We are amateur visual artists, posting photos on Instagram and pinning images on Pinterest. We expect to be participating in the conversation and not the target of a "message." This societal shift has contributed to the fall of traditional marketing mediums and forced the largest publishers, advertisers, and news channels to change their very core.

We appreciate businesses that understand this behavior and make our lives easier by creating paths to help us quickly and easily make our purchasing choices. This applies to all businesses across the board. Help your customers access the information they need when they need it and where they need it, and give them the tools to take action.

The traditional marketing channels are changing. We don't read glossy magazines like we used to. We tend not to subscribe to bulky print newspapers that will only accumulate in our recycle bins. We don't watch the commercials on our television programs as we often record programs on DVR or we watch streaming programming. We sign up on the national registry to stop junk mail from jamming our mailboxes and piling up in our landfills. When was the last time you used a print phone book? We listen to commercial-free digital playlists and streaming music more often than we tune into traditional radio stations. And, when we're waiting for a bus, riding public transportation, or otherwise experiencing a moment of downtime, we're most likely not paying attention to the environmental ads around us because we're busy checking our email or scanning Facebook.

Another complication with traditional advertising is that it's difficult to know what's working and what isn't. What's the first thing a business owner asks? "How did you hear about us?" They want to know how their advertising dollars are working and how best to direct efforts and spend in the future.

Traditional marketing campaigns cannot be quickly fine-tuned either. If you create a print ad or television campaign and run it, that's it. You can't test results and react instantly to optimize spending and reaction. With traditional marketing, you make a choice and hope for the best. Traditional campaigns are not sharable; there is no chance of a yellow pages advertisement going viral. No one shares a billboard. They are not directed to customers at the moment of decision. They cannot even be acted on immediately. They are limited to the information contained with the campaign and cannot link to other platforms, inspire interaction, or offer multiple ways to interface with customers. Traditional ads don't provide options for instant customer services. Traditional ads cannot establish a call to action allowing the customer to make a purchase in the moment. Traditional campaigns do not offer feedback or analytics or insight into your customer's habits or their path to conversion.

Old school marketing is going the way of the horse and buggy – it's a quaint relic of days gone by.

□ □ □

3. We Can Only Go Forward

You can only go forward. We're not going back. For most consumers, the mobile phone is a lifeline. It's hard to imagine what we did before we had mobile devices.

Being able to call for help from the phone in our pocket is something we take for granted. We connect with the people we love. We can use a smartphone's video camera and microphone to Facetime or Skype with relatives, coworkers, and friends we might not otherwise be able to see. We share videos and photos. We call and email. We expand our networks and social circles through social media. Mobile phones are a source of entertainment. They can inform purchases and can convert a passive activity to an interactive one.

On mobile devices we stay in touch with what's happening in our communities and the world. We respond to news and conversations and share ideas. We're not passive consumers of information; we are curators and commentators. We cultivate a voice with blogs and social media. We share our message. We pose questions, share ideas, and inspire conversation. We access information and we take college classes. We watch videos that teach us how to do everything from change the oil in our cars to learn the latest dance moves.

It wasn't long ago that we got our news from newspapers. They were printed once daily and tossed onto our doorsteps or we picked them up on the way to work. It's hard to imagine or remember when we weren't getting news on a twenty-four hour news cycle. We are kept abreast of events from around the world instantly and constantly. And we don't solely rely only on journalists and big newspapers. Citizens are informing and interacting in real time from mobile devices around the world.

Mobile has changed everything.

> ## Mobile has changed everything.

Mobile makes businesses accessible to individuals. Mobile meets customers where they are. It is of the moment, meaningful, and immediately actionable.

Are you going to be there for all this?

Your customers are mobile. Are you ready to be where they are when they need you? Are you ready to anticipate, meet and even exceed their expectations?

We reach for our mobile phone at the point of inspiration.

We're not just talking about phones, either. Mobile marketing applies to tablets as well. Use of tablets continues to grow with consumers and provides us with new ways to connect digitally. Larger than a mobile phone and smaller than a laptop computer, tablets are steadily gaining in popularity. Fourteen percent of mobile subscribers in the US own tablets, and that doesn't count e-readers including the Kindle Fire. Fifty-five million iPads were sold in the first eighteen months after introduction, 55,000,000.

Tablets offer greater portability while retaining the functionality of a computer. Cloud based software makes it easy for tablet owners to use their devices for almost everything they can do on their laptop or desktop computer. The larger screen size increases usability and makes navigating between functions and applications easier than on a mobile phone. This is especially true of older people and those with impaired vision.

Tablets are reaching critical mass. It took less than two years to reach nearly forty million tablets subscriptions in the U.S. It took smartphones seven years to reach that same level.

□ □ □

Interestingly, tablets are not replacing mobile phones or computers; they're being used as an additional screen. People are integrating tablets into their homes and workplaces. Wifi connections drove 40.3 percent of mobile Internet connections and 92.3 percent of tablet Internet connections in the United States. The increasing number of wifi hot spots and availability of internet connections in community places like libraries, coffee shops, and on public transportation have spurred the adoption of tablets.

Are you ready to reach out and be reached by customers on their mobile devices? If it makes sense to communicate with your audience, it makes sense to have a mobile marketing plan.

□ □ □

4. Immerse Yourself in Mobile Marketing

Mobile has become such an integral part of the way we navigate the world that we don't always notice the pockets of time people fill by taking out their mobiles.

When we discuss tactics we'll talk more about the specifics of how people are using their smartphones and tablets. But you can collect some anecdotal evidence on your own as well.

Next time you're waiting in a line at the grocery store or picking your kids up from camp, look around. Are people talking to each other or are they checking their email? When do you use your mobile device and when do you see people around you using theirs?

We use our mobile devices for everything from checking facts in the middle of real-life conversations to staying in touch with our business associates and planning our leisure activities. We search for answers: Did Tom Cruise ever win an Oscar? What is the distance between Dallas and Denver? What movies are playing at my local movie theatre? Do I have a meeting tomorrow afternoon? Are there any tennis courts available Saturday morning? How late is Whole Foods open? Where's the trailhead to that hike I wanted to take? What are my friends on social media up to? What are the headlines today? We take actions: I think I'll send these cute pictures of my kids/dog/lunch to my mom. I want to share this opinion piece from the *Times* with my friends. I want to check my bank balance – pay my cable bill – trade some options. I should reply to this email from my partner. You get the idea.

We've trained ourselves to manage the details of our lives constantly and from any place with a cell signal or wifi connection.

As we'll be talking about many different tactics on mobile devices, I'm going to suggest that you experiment with your own phone or tablet and get familiar with the possibilities. I'll lead you through this chapter by chapter, but in the meantime, when you come across ways that other companies and individuals are using mobile for marketing purposes, explore and learn what you think is working and what isn't.

To become familiar with the possibilities, experiment with your own mobile. Scan some QR codes when you come across them in print ads or in-store signage and consider what is useful about the page they direct you to. Do they give the customer valuable information that will ultimately add value and increase loyalty? Once you start thinking about them, you'll see QR codes in the most unexpected places. Take a minute and scan, and then think about which scans were worth the time and effort. Did that action bring you closer to the brand?

Sign up to receive short message service (SMS/Text Messages) messages from some favorite brands. How often do they text and what information is included in the message? Is it actionable? It is useful? It's easy to unsubscribe from SMS text marketing campaigns, so don't hesitate to experiment. As part of this research process, pay attention to what benefits companies are offering their customers in exchange for permission to contact them. Notice how the interruption of SMS text inspires you to action and if the information they share is timely and targeted. Are some of the campaigns using video or connecting to social media? How do the SMS interactions inspire conversation and interaction?

Ask friends and customers how they use their mobile devices. Get some recommendations for favorite applications. How is mobile making the lives of people you know easier? What can you learn from them? Study the habits of the people around you and be alert to the types of tasks they complete on their mobile devices.

Use location based services to find a coffee shop or another brick and mortar businesses around you. Conduct some local searches and notice the way businesses are ranked. Are mobile optimized sites listed first? Do these sites feature useful information such as store hours, the address and contact phone number?

Redeem a mobile coupon in a brick and mortar store. Try to use both a coupon from an application as well as one sent by SMS. Was the cashier trained to process the transaction smoothly? Would you be likely to use a mobile coupon again? Visit online retailers and compare their desktop sites with mobile versions. Download some apps from businesses and pay attention to whether the applications seem to be useful and engaging. Learn how other marketers are using mobile to build their brand, influence an audience, and increase sales.

Pay close attention to calls to action (CTA). What are marketers and online brands asking of the consumer? How do they inspire action? How did they get your permission to reach out to you? What did they offer? Did you feel closer to the brand after taking action? Would you be willing to share your positive (or negative) experience on a social networking site?

Understanding what other businesses are doing will help inform and inspire your own marketing decisions. While you'll want to be innovative in your campaigns, there is no reason not to learn from a consumer's perspective what works and what doesn't.

5. Testing Mobile Strategies

The opportunity in mobile marketing is enormous. But you already know that. It won't surprise you to hear that people spend more time using media features on mobile devices than they do reading newspapers and magazines combined (*eMarketer*).

While mobile marketing is in its infancy, it already has a huge presence in the way we live. There's little chance of people reverting to a less mobile lifestyle now that they've become accustomed to always being accessible and having access to information in the moment and in any environment.

Creating and implementing a mobile campaign is much more possible and simple than you might think. You don't need to be a heavy-duty programmer to have a huge impact in mobile. The strategies and tactics we're going to discuss in the upcoming sections are code-free. If you can post to Facebook or publish a blog, you can do this.

More than an appetite for innovation, you need a willingness to be flexible. Mobile gives you the opportunity to be nimble. You can start small and test everything. You'll know if it's working because it will convert almost immediately. Everything you do in mobile will be instant to test. And if it's not working, you have the opportunity to experiment, test the market and try something new.

The mobile marketing campaigns you create are going to be easy to target and track, and they'll serve your customers in a manner that's convenient to them. Marketing with mobile is not going to cost you an arm and a leg either. An SMS campaign can be set up in minutes and can cost pennies. Mobile has so many advantages over traditional marketing methods and it's really no risk at all to trial a campaign. As you will be able to instantly track results, you'll know how your marketing budget is working for you. There is no wait-and-see guesswork.

We already know why traditional isn't working so let's talk about what it takes to create a meaningful mobile marketing campaign.

You have to have a strong desire to reach customers where they are and be passionate about serving them. If you're willing to experiment a little, and to listen and adapt in order to best meet the needs of your customer, you've got what it takes to succeed in mobile marketing.

Your mobile tactics should reinforce your objectives to build your business. It's tempting to get sidetracked with mobile and all aspects of digital marketing. There are so many fun options! And delighting your customers can be a valid and important part of an overall marketing strategy. But, in mobile, it's important to stay on task and be sure that all communication and customer interface options reinforce the look and feel of the brand as well as the overall message.

When approaching a mobile campaign, it's makes sense to leverage the specific benefits and features of mobile and not treat it as you would static advertising such as print ads or passive advertising like television commercials. Don't just create ads as you would for print. Offer opportunities for interaction using social media, contests, and other CTA's.

Mobile devices are essentially pocket-sized computers, and yet in some ways their benefits exceed those of desktop machines in that they are more dynamic, responsive and location-specific. The cross-channel opportunities based on these features are important to realize. A customer can move seamlessly from an email to a mobile web page, or can place a call directly to customer service. He or she can map your location or post directly to social media. Also, like social media, it can be a starting point for a customer's journey closer to your brand. Therefore, communication can and should be rich and layered, and offer the customer multiple ways to interact and access information.

5. Testing Mobile Strategies

Mobile marketing is easy to analyze and adapt. Response rates, message delivery, click throughs, and sales conversions rates can all be tracked accurately, allowing maximum optimization and understanding of a campaign's success.

Mobile marketing is instant. We check our mobiles regularly and are used to seeking out pertinent and timely information from mobile devices. Local authorities have had great success sending out emergency updates such as evacuation notices for floods and fires, and information about power outages and traffic emergencies. Consumers are much more likely to quickly respond to information on their mobile device than if they were to hear an announcement on the radio or television, see a print advertisement or even get an email on their desktop. Mobile tends to lead to action instantly. If a customer receives communication from your brand, he or she can react immediately as he or she can gather more information, make a purchase, or respond to a call to action.

Marketers will benefit from leveraging the unique benefits of mobile. But, just as no single marketing tactic should be seen as an entire program, mobile should be part of an overall marketing strategy. You wouldn't just purchase space on a billboard and hope to grow a business from there. Nor would you only buy an ad in the yellow pages. Your social media presence can't build your brand alone without a path to engagement and the same is true for mobile marketing.

6. Opportunities in Mobile

Mobile marketing tactics can be easily integrated with other marketing channels to create a comprehensive strategy and to engage customers where they are. In fact, mobile makes it easy to seamlessly incorporate technology and to provide a positive customer experience by providing multiple options for engagement.

There is no reason to create only one path to conversion for customers. There are many possibilities to interact with and engage your customers, to spark conversations, and share useful content. Creating choices in the way customers can engage your brand is another opportunity to serve your customer and meet their needs.

Because mobile devices transition between features smoothly, they lend themselves to highly functional strategies. A mobile website might have a feature to find the nearest location of a retail outlet, and by using the location services of the mobile device the nearest store is located and mapped. Mobile websites can link to social media or to other event websites. A QR code can direct the consumer to a map, video, or a downloadable app. A mobile email might have a click to call feature. A social media post might direct to a mobile website or video. A SMS message can have a short link to a mobile commerce app or store. The possibilities and opportunities are endless.

Mobile marketing also plays well with traditional marketing as well as in-store experiences. Signs in stores can offer customers the opportunity to opt-in for useful SMS messages or to join a loyalty program. Customers can redeem coupons from their mobile phones either in stores or on a mobile commerce site. A billboard might feature a short code that directs to a mobile video and a television commercial can offer an SMS call to action.

Integrating mobile marketing as part of an overall strategy allows for mobile interactions to operate independently as well connect to other marketing methods. For example, a mobile email or text can have a link to a mobile site or a video, an opt-in page, a coupon, an invite to an in-store promotion, or anything that is the next step in the path of engagement.

In order to bring customers closer to your brand it's important to consider that there will not be one single path, as there will likely be various points of entry. A customer's first digital impression may originate from social media or an organic or paid search, or they may scan a QR code or opt-in to a short code that they came across in a print ad or in-store signage. Every interaction gives you the opportunity to win over the customer by anticipating and meeting his or her needs and engaging in a way that paves the way for the next interaction.

Mobile campaigns are affordable, and for a very small investment can be implemented in concert with other channels you're already using. The commitment doesn't need to be significant in order to start testing campaigns and seeing results. Because campaigns are so trackable, you'll seamlessly understand how best to direct your efforts.

Here's a cost comparison between SMS and direct mail.

DIRECT MAIL

Timing: One month + for ideation & design.

Design cost: Approximately $500.

Printing: Approximately $550 for 5,000 two-sided oversized postcards on most web based services.

Mailing services: Approximately $2,850 to send out those 5,000 postcards if you use your own list. Add approximately $300 if you're renting a list from the mailing service provider.

Delivery time: 5-12 business days

Conversion rate: If you saw a one percent conversion rate (which is tough today) that would equate to fifty new customers.

Total cost: $4,200.

Cost of customer acquisition: $84 per new customer.

Total time to start seeing results: Minimum six weeks.

SMS Marketing

Timing: On demand.

Design cost: Zero.

Delivery cost: $125 for 5,000 at 2.5 cents each (costs vary from 1.5 to 3.5 cents each based on volume).

Delivery time: Instant.

Conversion rate: Mobile conversion rates have been shown to be ten times that of direct mail, but for comparison sake we'll say the conversion rate stays the same at one percent and therefore you generate fifty new customers.

Total cost: $125.

Cost of customer acquisition: $2.50 per new customer.

Total time to start seeing results: Minutes.

> ## Mobile conversion rates have been shown to be ten times that of direct mail

This is just one example of why mobile marketing is not an option– it is imperative to your sustainable success.

When you market on mobile, you're marketing in real time. A mobile device is extremely versatile; it can take photos and videos and send them anywhere in the world, instantly. Most devices know where you are, and some understand which direction you are facing. A smartphone can answer your questions, call you mother, manage your finances, and store your important documents. Customers are used to being able to quickly search to locate the closest branch of a store and map it. They rely on their mobile devices to help them find solutions in the moment and to inform decisions as well as to complete transactions. If we need a gas station, we expect our mobile to locate one, immediately. Mobile devices are the ultimate business tool and life management system. Everything about mobile is related to instant access and meeting the immediate needs of the user.

The opportunities are huge. But, with so many options, it's not surprising that companies don't know where to start.

As you begin to think about your mobile campaign remember that all communication via mobile needs to be timely and relevant. If you're a restaurant, don't send an SMS or push notification from your app at 10am to promote a happy hour special. Send it at 4pm when people are starting to think about leaving work. Giving them an easy option is good business and keeps your brand top of mind.

6. Opportunities In Mobile

□ □ □

Every interaction you have with your customer on mobile should be able to be completed on the mobile device. If you send a mobile email with a link to a website, the website should be optimized for mobile. All calls to action should be simple to complete, specific, and useful to the consumer, as well as move the customer one step closer to your brand.

Keeping in mind the way that we use our mobile devices and how that is different from how we might use a desktop computer is an important piece of planning your mobile marketing strategy. It's about short, quick, easy to understand communication that's relevant and creates convenience for your customers. Making it easy for your customers to react to your messages is better for them and better for your bottom line.

□ □ □

7. Reaching Out in the Real World

There is no downtime. We are quickly shifting towards a lifestyle that's constantly connected. People pick up their mobile devices to fill brief pockets of wait-time and understanding how we tend to use mobile devices will influence how you create your campaigns.

We are always connected.

In a survey by Ericson consumer labs in 2011, 40% of the individuals surveyed said that it's important to them to be able to check their mobile devices first thing in the morning *while they're still in bed*. That's before they brush their teeth, exercise, or make that first cup of coffee. And a shocking 64% said they check their mobile devices from bed as the last thing they do at night before going to sleep. And that was in 2011. It's almost as if we're nervous something is going to happen without us during those eight hours of sleep.

And how about on a flight? You know the scene. The plane has landed. The fasten seatbelt light has just been turned off. The doors aren't yet open – and suddenly everyone has their cell phones out. They are texting. They are checking email. They're calling their loved ones to say, "We've landed safely."

We have reached a point in our history when we're always connected.

IMPERATIVE

□ □ □

We do more than one thing at a time. Not only are we regularly performing real-world activities and using our mobiles at the same time, we interact with more than one screen at a time! It's not at all uncommon for someone to be watching TV and using their mobile device, or checking text messages while using their desktop computer. We are becoming consummate multi-taskers. Half of all smartphone and tablet users report that they regularly check their email while watching TV. Forty-four percent said that they keep up with social networking while watching television. When a television program is running, 19% will look up coupons and deals at the same time (*Nielson*). No wonder cinemas have those irritating animated reminders to turn off devices during movies!

The propensity to not only always be connected but to do more than one thing at a time is interesting from a marketing perspective. We need to understand that our customers may have other input competing for their attention.

We're curious, but forgetful. We expect to be able to access information at any time and in any place. We may also be less likely to plan ahead, knowing we can check movie times after dinner. Before leaving home we don't bother to consult a map because we trust that the GPS on our mobile devices will help us find our location. When we can't remember the title of that book we wanted to read, it's easy enough to Google it. We're learning to rely on our mobile devices to answer our questions and solve our problems. We're a little more impulsive because we're able to be. We can decide where and when to meet our friends after work by texting them at the last minute.

Instant access to information affects not only our expectations but also the way people access and store information. There is some evidence that it's changing the way our minds work. A recently published paper, "Google Effects on Memory: Cognitive Consequences of Having Information at Our Fingertips" by Betsy Sparrow, Jenny Liu, and Daniel M. Wegner explores the question of whether people who know they can instantly locate information at a later date lose the desire (and ability) to store information. Evidence shows that this is indeed the case. If people believe they don't need to remember, they don't. As we become better at searching, our ability to recall may actually be diminishing.

We are all unique. Another compelling aspect of mobile devices is that they are highly customizable. Think of how much you can learn about someone by looking at the way they've arranged the tiles on their smartphone. Users determine how they will use their mobiles and for what purpose. In the most basic sense, they can glance at the device when they choose to. But the possibilities for customization go far beyond that. Users change the settings to alert them when a message or email comes through, or they can silence the device entirely. They give permission to the people and companies they want to be touched by.

If you have a smartphone, take a look at your first page of app tiles. What does your arrangement of features and apps say about you and the way you use your phone?

We organize our smartphones and tablets based on what is salient to us, and generally keep the most pertinent tiles in the front. Do you have your social media applications on the first page? Your camera? Do you have a weather app or an application to check sports scores? Have your children downloaded games? Is there an organizational app? Maybe you have a game that you enjoy. Do you have your music on the first page, or is it further back?

Later, we'll talk about creating customer personas and considering ways to reach out to your specific customers where they are and offering what they need and want.

□ □ □

Plan

□ □ □

The old adage is, "Fifty percent of my marketing is working – I just don't know which half." The trackability of mobile marketing and other digital marketing methods changes that.

□ □ □

8. Establishing a
Mobile Strategy

C reating an app is not a strategy. Neither is setting up a Facebook page, starting a blog, creating a website, taping a television commercial, buying radio time, or running a print ad.

Those are all tactics.

In any marketing plan, you need to create a dynamic and measurable strategy and implement it with meaningful tactics.

You will need to create a clear strategy with specific goals and objectives. Not only can mobile elements of your marketing strategy work together with other digital elements, but they can integrate with traditional marketing practices to form a comprehensive marketing strategy.

We have the opportunity to transform passive activities into opportunities for interaction. Someone sitting on the sofa watching *American Idol* becomes engaged as he or she texts in a vote. The customer is in a very real way a participant in the program. His or her vote is counted, and it matters when a winner is selected or a contestant is voted out. Customers can participate in surveys or scavenger hunts and you can offer loyalty programs that reward your customers for making purchases, interacting, or sharing information about your brand. You can create content that makes your customers look and feel good and that they wish to share, as well as design features, videos, or copy that is entertaining and sharable.

Give customers the opportunity to comment and create conversations of their own. Consider opportunities for customer created content and give the people who are interacting with your brand the opportunity to express themselves.

Creating goals that define what you want to accomplish and the steps that you'll take to get there is the first step in crafting a strategy.

Each interaction should be of value to the consumer and draw him or her closer to your brand. Consider it relationship building.

Fortunately, in the realm of mobile, all businesses – regardless of size – are starting from the same place. We are all trying to determine how best to reach and engage our customers. In order to create an effective campaign, a company must provide value to the consumer. In the short term this can be as simple and clear as a discount or coupon. Eventually, your customers will expect you to be a resource, to make their lives easier, and to be a brand with which they can identify.

A mobile strategy needs to be measurable. In the end your goals are to increase sales and to build customer relationships. Establishing goals and measuring tactics to determine how effective they are just makes sense. With digital marketing, and specifically mobile, it's so easy to track and adjust campaigns and there is no reason not to do so. But you can't make informed changes if you don't understand what's working and what isn't.

□ □ □

9. The True Market Test

Bringing your campaign to market is the true test.

First, you'll want to consider your target audience and what makes them tick, and then launch a well-planned and thought-out strategy. To borrow the familiar shampoo slogan, you'll want to track, listen, rinse, and repeat.

Once you have listened to your customers, learned what is working and what is not, and you have anticipated how to better meet their needs and engage them where they are, create a small campaign and test it in the real world. This doesn't have to cost much money and the potential return on investment (ROI) is great. There is no need to jump into a huge launch. Test the market and learn from customer's reactions.

In his book *The Lean Start-Up*, Eric Ries encourages entrepreneurs to adopt an approach he characterizes as "build-measure-learn." The same approach is viable with mobile marketing campaigns. He doesn't suggest that entrepreneurs just throw a product out there in the market without doing any research. Instead, Ries suggests that entrepreneurs ask themselves questions about their product and their customers, and how best they can meet their customers' needs. We talked about similar questions when we discussed understanding your customers.

After understanding the problem you aim to solve and your customers he suggests creating a minimum viable product or MVP, and putting it out there in the world in order to commence the process of learning and adapting. He takes a scientific approach to product development that can be applied to marketing as well.

Create a minimum viable campaign that aligns with the information you have about your customers and applies to your marketing strategy. And then measure your key performance indicators and identify your actionable metrics. Don't get overwhelmed with all the possible analytics. Instead, focus on the metrics that you can take additional action from, learn from the results and adapt your campaigns accordingly.

The benefit of the build-measure-learn approach is not simply that it's less costly, though it is. When applied to mobile marketing campaigns, feedback will also be almost instant. But the true benefit of the approach is that you can apply an organized and informed method to marketing based on the behaviors and preferences of your actual customers and future customers. There's no guesswork involved.

10. Your Target Audience

Focus groups stink.

Old school marketers and advertising agencies relied on focus groups for customer feedback, and some still do. A mediator armed with questions from the brand and strategic team gathers a group of individuals from a specific demographic and tries to ascertain their opinions, preferences, and biases related to a particular brand, industry or product.

But focus groups are flawed in many ways. The questions are predetermined. The group has been selected based on what the strategists expect to hear and who they believe their audience will be. In some cases, specifically when administered by an amateur, the questions are asked in a way to elicit the kind of response the strategists expect. They aren't looking for surprises, outliers, or the unexpected insight that comes from organic or natural testing.

New media marketing allows for real world analytics. Like sociologists, we can learn how applications are actually used, not how we think they might be or how customers think they would use them, but how they are actually used. Remember that advertisers used to employ a project-out message. They were trying to convince customers that they needed the product or service they were offering and that their particular brand was the one the customers should choose. Advertising used to be about persuasion. Marketing was focused on convincing an audience to believe your message.

But that has changed. As people become more and more vocal, they create their own circles of influence. They layer their opinions, uses, and biases onto the messages of the marketers. They are influencers and expect to create content and not passively consume it.

Focus groups generally have two stages, and both can be replaced and improved upon by using new media strategies. Focus groups are generally first used to gain insight into the market and the thoughts, needs, and desires of potential customers. Then, once a campaign has been developed, focus groups can offer opinions on the customer experience and preferences regarding the message as well as the visual look and feel of the program. New media and mobile marketers can gain insight testing a campaign and responding to audience feedback quickly and with minimal expense.

In addition to being quick and inexpensive, market testing strategies create a more accurate measure of real-world opinion and true customer behavior.

Imagine a company whose brand of toothpaste occupies a solid share of the market. They have a new product in development and want to position it in the marketplace. But, first they want to know what people think about toothpaste in general. They form focus groups and conduct interviews asking people chosen from a specific demographic about their dental hygiene habits. They divide users into three groups based on their feelings and experience with dental care. Some are focused on their teeth because they believe a bright smile is part is an important part of being attractive. Some focus on dental health and want to maintain the overall health of their teeth, but are not as concerned about appearances. The last group is afraid of potential problems they might have with their teeth if they are neglected and their dental care choices are focused on avoiding negative consequences of not brushing.

The company then spends months on additional focus groups and learns what you might have already guessed – that most people fall into the second category. They then decide to target this group of people for their next campaign with the intention of nudging them up towards the first group by convincing them that having a brighter smile will make them feel better about themselves, increase their confidence, and make them more attractive, and they will also maintain good dental health in the process.

Next, the company marketing team brainstorms some names. They take the names to focus groups. They create some prototype packaging. Back to focus groups.

Then they experiment with flavors. More focus groups.

They come up with a brand strategy. Focus groups.

They create a choice of three tag lines. Focus group.

They get some images from creative. Focus group.

They decide they want to know how people in group number two feel about social media. Focus group.

They wonder if they would be willing to connect with their brand on the internet. Focus group.

They test a specific campaign and ask for feedback. Focus group.

This process takes time and money and is all done by large and inefficient committees, who already know what they want the numbers to support before they even begin to design the products and campaigns around these assumptions.

When you're in the early stages of designing a campaign, you might be better off analyzing real-life feedback avenues such as Twitter for a while and see how people are talking about your product. Learn the way people discuss topics related to your industry. Pay attention to their concerns and their praise. Go to social media to research trends and the way that individuals encounter your brand as well as those of your competitors.

Once you have some ideas of how to implement your campaign, consider A/B testing. Create two options and send them to a small portion of your list, post them on social media, or distribute in a small way. Then, watch the analytics. This can be done with everything from an email to a mobile website. See how customers react. What is the open rate? How long do they spend on the page or site? Do they follow through on your CTA? What is the conversion rate?

You can also learn a lot by paying attention to how customers come to you in the first place. With analytics, you can not only see where they were just prior to coming to your page, but you can go back through several steps towards conversion. You can learn if your customers are coming from searches or social media, or if they visited a blog or encountered a brand ambassador. You'll learn which marketing efforts are working and which aren't as useful.

Defining your target audience in order to anticipate their needs and better engage with them is a strategic way to add value and can (and should) inform positioning, promotions and strategy decisions.

Writers often create an imaginary reader when deciding how best to create a narrative and tell a story. As the goal of the writer is to entertain, enlighten, and delight (as well as to sell more books), they write with the reader in mind. It also helps to create a persona because it makes the audience more specific and it's easier to anticipate the needs and desires of the reader.

Creating customer personas will help you create meaningful paths to conversion, anticipate needs, and target your campaigns to your specific customer base.

By using the data you have already collected about your customers, it's likely you already know something about them. But you can expand on this and create customer personas to inform your marketing campaigns.

Some of the features of your customers' personas should be:

✓ Age

✓ Gender

✓ Specific location: Geographical factors (e.g., region or country, urban or rural).

✓ Technical comfort: Computer experience - what devices do they use? How does he or she use them?

✓ What mobile devices do they use and how do they use them?

✓ Education

✓ Job title

✓ Income

✓ Backstory (a little about their lives)

Once you have established a little bit about their personalities, consider where and how they may likely interact with your brand:

✓ Motivations. What concerns do they have – why do they need this product or service?

✓ Frustrations. What is stopping them from choosing this product or service?

✓ Environment of experience. Relevant characteristics of the environment in which the product/service will be used.

✓ Walk through typical experience. What was he or she doing before – what will he or she be doing after? What else is vying for their time?

✓ Goal. What is the customer's objective for interaction? What are secondary benefits?

✓ Ideal experience. What features will solve their problems and enchant or delight to give them the most positive experience?

✓ Attitude and expectations. What attitudes and expectations might influence their experience?

You need to remember that personas are illustrations of your target customer segments. You could have two or twenty different customer personas based on your business and scope of products or services you offer.

I highly recommend giving each persona a face and name as well. This makes it more real and allows you to see each as a real customer rather than a bunch of data. Some companies have even gone as far as to create a cardboard cutout of their personas and place them around the office to remind employees who it is they are serving and what's important to them. It sounds corny, but it works.

Understanding the habits of your current customers is an important aspect of developing a robust and successful mobile marketing campaign. By checking the analytics on your current site you'll be able to find out how your customers are accessing your site and which platforms they are using.

Ask yourself:

1. What platforms do my customers use?

2. What platforms do the customers who are most loyal use?

3. What platforms will my potential customers use?

4. How are my current / best/ potential customers using their phones and tablets?

It used to be an important question to ask what percentage of your customers have and use smartphones. Now, it's understood that nearly everyone is using smartphones and those who aren't will be doing so very soon.

Don't just ask which tablets and smartphones they are using; consider the other channels that might be important to your customers. Are they using Facebook and updating their statuses regularly? Are your customers tweeting? Are they using Instagram or Pinterest? How can you best reach them now and how might you serve them better in the future?

□ □ □

11. Messaging Strategy

Be considerate of your customer's time. Consider both the timing of your message and the length of time it will take out of your customer's day. Plan the interaction to occur within the set amount of time one tends to allot for a quick phone check. Consider the amount of time your dining companion takes to go to the rest room, or how long you wait at the deli counter. Most of these activities take only a few minutes. You want your message to be brief and simple enough that your customers can complete the call to action as quickly as possible and continue down your relationship-building path.

If your marketing is playful, useful, and appealing to customers, they might seek it out at a given time instead of checking Facebook, playing Angry Birds, or looking at the news headlines. It seems to me that all mobile interactions should be brief enough to be completed at the time the consumer first comes into contact with the message. For example, if we see a billboard we have to remember to call that number when we get home. How often do we remember? With email you might flag a message if there is a response needed. You might bookmark a webpage. But with mobile (and honestly, with everything), your best bet at getting a favorable result is to plan the interaction to occur within the amount of time one tends to allot for a quick phone check – just a couple minutes and preferably less.

IMPERATIVE

□ □ □

TIMING

It's important to consider the timing of your messages. A busy mom may not want to receive a message about making a haircut appointment in the evening when she's trying to figure out how to get dinner on the table for her family. However, she may be pleased to get a coupon for a last-minute special at a local restaurant.

Test your message timing and coordinate the content with the time of day. Be aware of the lifestyles of your target customers and present them with meaningful solutions at opportune moments. According to an Ericson study in 2011, lunchtime and early evening are the two most frequent times of day that Americans access the internet via smartphone.

Experiment. Choose a time that you think will be convenient for your customers and reach out. Test results and make any necessary adjustments.

It's also important to let customers decide how frequently they hear from you and over which channels they wish to interact. Give them options. Do they want push notifications? Text messages? Weekly email newsletters? Customers should be able to filter content to meet their needs and to be sure that all interactions are welcome, useful, and productive. Make it quick, convenient, relevant, and timely and your customers will thank you by staying connected and spreading their joy.

PHRASING

Many parents learn to phrase questions to their children in a way that no matter how the child responds, the parent gets a desired answer. "Would you rather take your nap and then have your snack or do you want to have snack first, then nap?" I'm not suggesting you treat your clients like toddlers, but it's wise to ask questions that give your customers the ability to respond in a way that gives them some agency. Perhaps something like, "Would you rather receive a ten percent discount or a free bagel on your next visit?" Options and ownership form a level of

44

subconscious partnership and allows your customers to feel like part of the decision making process and that much closer to your business.

BE A RESOURCE

We encounter messages constantly. Everyone is vying for our attention. People come into contact with more messages in a day than they can even process. It's your job to break through the noise and be the beacon of clarity with relevant solutions for your customers.

Send useful signals, not meaningless static. Don't overwhelm consumers with chatter. A good strategy is to do something different from what everyone else is doing. Stand out and learn to deliver what's needed in the time of need. With a little planning and measurement it can be done.

You might even offer solutions for sorting through the influx of messages on your topic. For example, curate information in your area of expertise or relating to your brand and become a resource that customers can turn to when they want solutions. We are overwhelmed with noise. At the most basic level, all interactions need to be permission-based. Clearly, you don't want your message to be spam. But there is more to it than that.

Become THE resource. Consider ways that you can present yourself or your business as a useful component of the filtering process. For example, if you're targeting dieters or health conscious consumers develop an app to filter the latest research on super foods or the latest cancer discoveries. Help your environmentally conscious customers be informed of the latest research on sustainably relevant products. Find ways to make life easier for your customers, to be a trusted resource and a positive source of useful information. Become THE solution.

INTERACTION

All mobile and social conversations should be two-way. Don't be a broadcaster. Give your customers a way to be heard. Invite interaction.

Offer ways to connect. Messages should be interactive and offer options for customers to engage with your message and company.

Content should be sharable. Creating energetic and fun content is a great way to engage customers. Your campaigns should increase brand value and make life easier for your audience while offering a certain level of entertainment, if at all possible. This is where fun, unique messaging comes in. It's not always about promotion. It's about a positive brand experience. Even if the brand is a side note to the core message.

> ## It's about a positive brand experience.

One of the best ways to meet your customers' needs is to ask them what they want. Get customers to let you know their preferences. Marketing campaigns based on insight into consumer habits and preferences will be the most targeted and have the greatest impact. Consumers are truly in control of the messages they receive and respond to on mobile. They can either delete your message with the touch of a finger or, with as much ease, they can share it with their entire network of friends.

You don't want to irritate customers with content that isn't targeted or relevant. Enchant your customers by anticipating their needs and only reaching out when you have something to offer them that will be useful and meaningful to them. Campaigns should be personalized and segmenting data is a great way to create groups with specific interests and needs. Then develop exclusive offers based on their preferences and watch your conversion rates jump.

Be available. Make it easy for customers to contact you and seek information. Have click to call or email buttons on your mobile site, in mobile optimized emails and on your company's mobile app. Be responsive to all incoming messages and diligent with social media. All conversations should be interactive and transparent. Remember not to broadcast out, but to invite dialogue. Your message should be sharable. Make your message appealing enough that people want to spread the word. Respect your customer's time and attention by offering easy to follow CTAs and simple ways to offer feedback such as comment sections or Facebook like buttons. Consider other ways to get quick and easy feedback from customers such as the simple buttons on Amazon and Trip Advisor that ask, "Was this review helpful?" Listen to your customers and let their voices and opinions guide your content. Learn by experimenting. Find out what is working for your customers and do more of that and less of what doesn't resonate. Marketing campaigns based on insight into consumer habits and preferences will have the greatest impact.

Always be looking for ways to make things simpler, easier, and more fun for your customers. You do the work so that they don't have to.

IDENTIFY LEADERS

It's important to identify influencers, bloggers, social media mavens, and business leaders relating to your topic, product, service, or industry. There are many ways to do this.

Stay on top of social media by monitoring popular networks and relevant keywords. You can use a program like HootSuite to organize your social media campaigns and alert you when certain keywords are used. Here are a few ways to do this on two popular social networks, Facebook and Twitter.

FACEBOOK

If you're using HootSuite you can easily set up each of your Facebook profiles and Pages in the HootSuite dashboard. This will give each account a tab in the dashboard so you can easily monitor your news feed.

Next make sure you've "Liked" the Pages or become Friends with the people who have cultivated the audience you want to attract (Some pages don't require this. It depends on the owner's settings). Add to the conversation and offer your opinion as well as ask relevant questions. The key is to add value and become part of the community. Start broadcasting promotions and you'll turn everyone off.

Lastly, simply monitor your news feed for appropriate opportunities to comment on or Like different posts. This is a great way to start getting your name or brand out in front of your target audience in a casual and natural way. On certain pages you can even be the one who starts the conversation. It all depends on the settings the page owner has in place.

Secret Tip: Don't use comments like "I agree," "what a great story," or "thanks for sharing." Add something to the conversation. Treat it like a real conversation you would have if you were face to face. People want to get to know you, the person or business, not robot brands.

TWITTER

Twitter is even easier to monitor in HootSuite. Once your accounts are setup in the system you'll have a tab on the dashboard for each account, just like I described for Facebook above. On your Twitter tab you can setup what they call Streams (columns in the dashboard for specific info). For instance, I have a stream that is just @Mentions of me, @BrettRelander. This allows me to see everyone who mentions me in an update and is a great opportunity for continued discussion and relationship building. You can also set up streams for lists you've created, other people's lists you're following, or specific keywords across all of Twitter. You don't even have to be following the people to see what they are saying. It's a great listening tool and allows you tremendous insight into specific industries or about specific products, services, brands, or events.

As a secondary option you can search the twittersphere at search. twitter.com or http://twitter.com/#!/search-home to see what's being said about any topic. Both will take you to the same place.

In addition to monitoring your social media accounts you can also update your social media accounts directly from the HootSuite dashboard. I currently monitor Twitter, Facebook, LinkedIn, and Google+ Pages with HootSuite, and they offer the ability to monitor other networks as well.

You can get the attention of thought leaders and influencers by mentioning them and responding to their social media posts. Interacting with bloggers by posting insightful comments to develop a rapport with them and most bloggers appreciate being emailed on occasion and hearing that their work is appreciated. This is a great opportunity to increase your social activity and participate in more conversations relating to your industry, brand, or product.

If someone mentions your product specifically, reply to them. Keep the conversation going. Show your gratitude and share your energy and passion for your product or topic. People appreciate it when companies reach out to them directly. It's a great way to show your appreciation, but also to establish yourself as responsive and engaged with your customers.

If there are people saying good things about you or your brand such as, "Had a great dinner at Mario's Restaurant last night." surprise them with a reply, Let them know how much you enjoyed having them. When appropriate, in order to further engage the customer you might consider asking questions. If they say, "I can't wait to get my new sneakers at Bob's shoes," you might respond, "We can't wait to see you. What style is your favorite?"

If someone posts a product from your site, such as, "I just got Fluffy this new collar!" Perhaps you could reply, "Thanks for coming in. It looks great on Fluffy!"

Active Listening

You can also learn a lot about your industry from the things people are saying in blogs and in social media. Do they have concerns that you can address? Are there other features that would be useful to them that you haven't considered? Invite feedback on your own social media pages as well. Let customers have a voice and contribute content. You will likely find that some have already selected themselves as brand ambassadors. You can empower them to continue to spread the word and even recognize or reward them for doing so.

IMPERATIVE

□ □ □

If you come across a negative comment that relates to your brand, do your best to make things right. Apologize and reach out in an attempt to solve the problem. Be real. Be humble. Be attentive.

People who are talking about your product and industry are perfect candidates to become brand ambassadors. You can reward brand ambassadors and brand champions with discounts, perks, or even special events. You also have the option to create a formal affiliate program where they are rewarded for referrals.

INFLUENCING THE INFLUENCERS

Bloggers and thought leaders are often sent products from manufactures and retailers in the hopes that they will use them in a future story. A food blogger may receive a chef's knife, a bottle of vanilla, or single source chocolate. If you do send product samples to the media and bloggers, it's best to ask them first in an email. (This is usually necessary in order for them to share their mailing address.) Understand that bloggers and the press won't guarantee they will write about your book, product or service, but they may get as excited about it as you are. You can follow up after they receive it and ask if they liked it, but don't ask them specifically to feature it on their site or in their print publication. That said, many bloggers and writers would be happy to receive and feature products that they find useful. Sending a new rolling pin to a popular cooking blogger with a nice note that says something like, "Thanks for all you do to inspire home bakers. We wanted you to have this new rolling pin from our new collection and hope that you'll enjoy it."

Developing mutually beneficial relationships is an inexpensive and very effective way to spread the word about your business and establish your brand in social media. Consider who has your same core audience, develop a list, and start reaching out.

Another way to build your audience is to reach out to bloggers and media specialists and ask to contribute to their site. You can offer them the chance to do so on yours as well. This can be done in an interview format or you can have them write on a specific topic. Whether you're contributing on someone else's blog or they're contributing on yours, you'll link to each other's sites and you'll be exposed to each other's audiences. This can be a very useful tactic for growing an audience and reaching a specific demographic of people who are interested in very targeted content. Please note the difference in contributing and guest blogging. Guest blogging has recently become frowned upon by Google so I suggest refraining from using the words "guest blogger" or "guest post" on your sites. Contributors should be niche specific and relevant to your area of expertise, industry, or product. The contributor should also have a profile on the site and a byline on the article.

MEASURE IT

Whatever you do in mobile, it's measurable. Everything. Whether you're accounting for the number of people clicking on an ad, responding to a marketing text message, redeeming a coupon, or downloading your app, you'll be able to access detailed analytics that will help you refine your mobile marketing campaigns and make them more effective and deliver the maximum return on investment.

Digital marketers have the ability to track every aspect of every campaign. You can easily learn what's working and what's not. You can understand the paths your customers are taking to reach you and what steps they take before making a purchase or connecting with your brand.

Tools like Google Analytics for mobile can break down the stats on your mobile site. Google Analytics can give you extensive information on landing pages for QR codes as well as video views, and customer pathways to conversion. There are analytics for mobile email that will let you know open rates, click throughs, as well as understand conversion rates and sales.

We have the ability on these channels to track customer behavior and to use that information to shape future campaigns in order to provide a better experience for your customers. Much of this goes back to customer flow and being able to identify the types of conversions that are valuable to a business. It's obvious that sales are valuable, but what about Facebook likes, Twitter followers, email subscribers, mobile subscribers, website traffic, shares on Facebook, and RTs on Twitter?

> ## It's important to take residual value into consideration when determining what to measure.

Useful measurement values go far beyond dollars and cents. It's important to take residual value into consideration when determining what to measure and when setting campaign goals. You want to know how you're influencing others with the understanding that their influence can in turn drive future sales. Can someone never purchase anything from you and still have value? Yes, because they can inspire others to take action.

Someone who has had a positive experience with your company's brand, product or service has more influence when speaking about it than messages coming directly from the company. Inspire others to gush. We tend to trust referrals of friends and thought leaders because their opinion feels more genuine.

Strategy is the most important aspect of any mobile campaign. I know it's tempting to get excited about cutting-edge and novel technologies such as near field communication (NFC), augmented reality (AR) and location-based services (LBS). My best advice is to keep your eye on your goals and don't get distracted at the beginning. You might be in a rush to implement the newest technology or commence an all-out mobile blast. But take a deep breath and design a strategy that is going to best help you achieve your business's goals. Begin by evaluating and learning about your customers, how they are currently using mobile, and how you can best meet them where they are. Clearly define your objectives. Do you intend to attract new customers or are you all about engaging your current customers and keeping them loyal? Will your brand be primarily a mobile brand or will your mobile campaigns be bridges to other channels and methods of interaction? Consider the ways that mobile can help you reach your goals and start small. It's always better to test and learn from campaigns and adapt as necessary. In this way you'll be able to wind up with a strategy that meets your customers' needs and resonates with them. This is your opportunity to literally be in the palm of your customer's hands. Don't miss it. Capture it!

Deploy

□ □ □

12. Mobile-Friendly Elements

Once you have established a strategy, the fun begins: you need to determine which mobile marketing channels make the most sense for your brand. You know your customers; you understand both how they are currently reaching you as well as an idea of ways that you might be able to better serve them. As you know, mobile devices offer many opportunities to connect with your customers. Finding the right methods and elements for your business and customers will be the next step

It's likely you already understand the most essential aspects of a mobile plan based on your own experimentation. I'm sure you've received an email that isn't formatted for easy reading on your mobile. And, if you're like most of us, you either deleted the email or tagged it to come back to it later. It's frustrating to try to read small font or have to expand and scroll for emails that simply won't load on a mobile device correctly. Reaching out to your customers with email that can be accessed from any device is just good business. Imbedding mobile-friendly features in the email such as hyperlinks for more information, videos, and paths to social media are simple ways to encourage communication and engagement.

Likewise, maybe you've had some challenges with websites that aren't mobile friendly. You just want to check the schedule at the gym or find out the store hours of your local coffee shop, but the sites were designed for the desktop, rather than with responsive design, and the fonts are too tiny to read. You try to click on a hyperlink and it's a quarter the size of the tip of your index finger, so you click on the wrong link and are slowly and tediously directed to an unintended page. It's a common and maddening experience. It's essential to make it as easy as possible for the customers who want to connect with you to do so. They shouldn't have to jump through hoops, squint at tiny print, or click through page after page to find the most basic information. Make it easy for customers to do business with you by maintaining a site that is mobile-friendly.

We'll talk about apps and SMS as well as QR codes. And it's important to look ahead and consider ways to use location, near field communication, push messaging, and fun features such as augmented reality to engage and delight your customers.

Mobile ad networks are exploding, and the costs and availability are manageable now. Getting a handle on how mobile users are seeking your products will indicate your strategy here.

Mobile payment processors include PayPal, Intuits GoPayment, Authorize.net, Google Wallet, or Square. Just know that there are good solutions now and even more on the horizon.

Near field communication (NFC) is increasingly available on mobile devices. When touching two devices together, information can be shared through a radio signal. I anticipate that in the near future there will be NFC simplified wifi connections in specific locations. Data can be exchanged between NFC users and there are interesting opportunities for commerce such as payment systems. Ticketing systems may also soon be available through NFC. Before you know it, you might be able to walk into a Ranger's game without ever taking a ticket or even your mobile device out of your pocket. Smartphones with NFC technology can be programmed to perform automated tasks such as send texts, videos and documents to others with NFC equipped smartphones that are tagged to receive the data. You can also make apps available via NFC. This technology creates opportunities for offering customers on-the-spot discounts, coupons, or insider information when they enter your store.

Augmented reality is still pretty new in the world of mobile and specifically in the small business market. But marketers are learning from game developers and are implementing augmented reality in their campaigns. A report from Juniper research indicates that AR technology generated more than two million dollars in sales in 2012, which is anticipated to climb to $714 million dollars by 2014. Marketers such as Moosejaw have been successful in creating augmented reality campaigns. And the 2013 IKEA catalog had a corresponding app that uses augmented reality to reveal hidden items and additional information relevant to the corresponding catalog page. Location-based AR is also an exciting frontier and will likely drive growth. AR is attractive and fun. And when things are fun, we tend to play with them a little longer. Marketers are looking for ways to engage and delight customers to foster positive brand associations. A healthy mix of both information and entertainment is a great way to get your customers attention, impress them, and give them something to talk about with their friends.

Sometimes, fun is the best tactic!

□ □ □

13. Customer Loyalty

Mobile strategies can be implemented to create and maintain customer loyalty programs. Instead of using a loyalty card to receive discounts or accumulate points towards free products, mobile devices can be used to check-in and manage programs. This offers a great deal more function over printed paper cards that customers might have hole-punched or the many key ring loyalty programs.

For example, your offer could be to buy ten frozen yogurts and get the eleventh free. Not only can you collect your customer's information at the beginning in order to offer additional discounts and alert them to promotions in the future, you're able to understand and analyze customer behavior through the data you collect. Mobile programs also are easier on consumers than keeping track of punch-card loyalty cards or scan-able cards that they must keep on their key chains or in their wallets. Grocery stores who are already keeping track of consumer preferences such as purchase history and styles can offer their customers ease of use by having loyalty programs linked to mobile instead of cluttering their wallets. Also, if marketers gain permission, there is the possibility of further contact whereby you can let customers know about promotions that are in alignment with their preferences or interests. You can also offer incentives to customers who haven't shopped in a while. Getting the customer's permission or enrolling them can be as simple as having them download your mobile app or send in a quick text.

Mobile is an excellent loyalty and customer relationship management (CRM) tool for businesses of all sizes. You don't have to be a national chain to implement a program that is useful for consumers and offers an impressive return on investment. By asking permission from existing and new customers you can integrate a program that meets their needs and simplifies their experience, and at the same time keeps your business in their minds (and on their mobile devices).

Customer loyalty programs can offer rewards for purchases, can remind customers of upcoming sales or promotions, or provide reminders to customers for service. A restaurant might let customers know if there is a happy hour special, dinner promotion or special event on a Tuesday evening when they don't have many reservations. A doctor, dentist, hairdresser, or other appointment-based professional can send out reminders when it's time for customers to schedule their next appointment. They can even offer options to schedule directly from their mobile app by having click-to-call or appointment scheduling features. In addition, they can offer convenience reminders the day before a scheduled visit, such as, "You have an appointment with Dr. Smith tomorrow at 9:00 a.m." via text. Salons can offer specials – "Friday afternoon blow-out special, $25.00." It's wise to include a CTA, or click to schedule feature. If you have a salon with empty chairs on a Friday afternoon, why not fill them with clients who would love to have their hair or nails done before the weekend.

14. Social Media Integration

Social media has changed the way we interact online. Sixty-six percent of online adults are connected to one or more social media platforms. Half of them say they check in with social media first thing in the morning, even before they get out of bed.

People increasingly use social networking sites not only to interact with their friends but also with brands and businesses. This platform will only grow in importance for marketers seeking to engage their social networking audiences through mobile with location-based services.

According to a 2011 Neilson study, thirty percent of US mobile consumers value social networking features on their phone. It's not surprising that social media continues to be the fastest growing mobile activity. Facebook is the number one app and 189 million of Facebook's users are 'mobile only.' People check their Facebook profiles and pages through their mobile's browser and the Facebook app as well as third party social media organizers such as HootSuite and TweetDeck. Individuals are projecting their opinions and preferences on social media and expect to be heard. Sometimes, one of the wisest things you can do as a marketer is to listen and to give your social media friends and followers opportunities to engage and to express themselves. Make your customers look good and feel good about their interactions with your company.

Mobile devices and social media go well together because mobile makes real time interactions with social media possible when users are away from their desks. With the ability to connect instantly and from anyplace, mobile users have made real-time social networking the norm. We see people updating statuses and tweeting during sporting events and while watching television programs. Consider the role that social media is playing in world events such as the Arab Spring, where citizens took to social platforms to organize themselves and share from-the-street information across their cities and across the world. And how about the #BringBackOurGirls initiative. You would have to be living in a cave to have missed this powerful and emotional campaign.

We see the way we use social media as a way to be current, instant, and in the know. We use it to share pictures of our children, our pets, or what we ate for dinner. We also use it as a means to give advice, pass on tips, discuss a newspaper article we just read, share a joke, and let friends know about the great restaurant you found. We invite friends to events using social media. We pass on valuable information. We send links to videos we enjoyed and we post videos we have created. Social media is a way to build a reputation, to share information, and to build community. We talk about the movies we see and the funny or vexing things we encounter. We tell the stories that inspire and delight us and we share that information instantly with our networks.

In one month alone – December 2011 – over sixty-four million U.S. smartphone users accessed social networking sites or blogs on their mobile devices at least once, with more than half of these mobile social networking users accessing social media almost every day, and that was in 2011. While mobile social networking users showed the highest propensity to read posts from people they knew personally, more than half of those also reported reading posts from brands, organizations, and events.

Not only do people use social media as way to project news and updates, we also scan the posts of our network of friends and companies. Social media has become a news and entertainment aggregator and a filter for information. While in years past most people might have found your business by an advertisement or search, it's likely that today many of your customers' first point of contact originates from social media.

Content should be useful or fun. It should add value and be sharable and help build your own reputation as well as be good for the people who pass it on.

Social media offers unparalleled opportunities for customer service as well. You can reply to customers who post about your brand or product and offer solutions, insight or gratitude. You can use social media to mention loyal customers and engage them. Social media is an opportunity to expand your reach and to reinforce relationships with your audience. It can be at the same time universal and personal.

A successful social media campaign establishes a way to create a narrative, share your passion for your product, service and customers, offer solutions, and start conversations. You can create excitement around your brand. You can get instant feedback on social media if you ask customers a question, thereby giving your customers a voice and agency in your brand. Remember that marketing is no longer about talking to an audience and telling them what they need; it's about listening, interacting, and delivering what they want.

When considering ways to connect with customers via mobile, be willing to investigate and experiment with a variety of social media platforms. Brands such as Urban Outfitters, Tiffany and Company, Redbull, Jetblue, and Burberry are using Instagram to engage their audience with visually appealing content and find out what resonates. This type of experimentation leads to valuable insights and increased success over time as well as an opportunity to build relationships with their customers.

Include a CTA in social media. Only 26% of businesses frequently include a CTA in tweets and 49% never do. That's a lost opportunity. A CTA can be as simple as asking customers to like or share, vote, provide feedback, or check out a video. It doesn't, and shouldn't in most cases, be sales based. The call to action should be mobile friendly, as it's likely customers will be accessing social media platforms with their mobile devices.

As of January 2014, Twitter had 645 million active registered users. Twitter users send 58 million tweets each day and 135,000 new accounts are added each day.

Facebook has over 1.3 billion users and 48% of all users log in daily and 31% percent of Facebook users check in more than once a day.

LinkedIn has over 300 million users, and an amazing 72 million visit LinkedIn every day. Half of LinkedIn users have a bachelor's degree or higher.

Google+: Has over 310 million users and 20 million unique mobile monthly users.

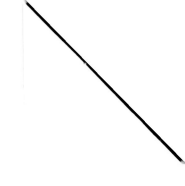

□ □ □

15. Mobile Commerce

If you have something to sell (who doesn't?) and you're not considering mobile in your marketing plan, you're missing an opportunity to
connect with motivated customers who are close to the point of decision. Mobile has transformed the way we think about shopping. Sixty-
four percent of smartphone owners make purchases from their mobile
devices. (Source: eDigitalResearch and Portaltech Reply, 2012) Mobile
shoppers are ready to act now and they tend to use their mobile devices
for task-related searches and not just to pass time.

The Mobile Path to Purchase survey conducted by Nielson in 2012
revealed some exciting results for mobile commerce. The study revealed
that 51% of mobile auto searchers and 46% of mobile travel searchers ultimately make a purchase. The study also discovered that 87% of mobile
searches for restaurants were made by consumers who were planning on
dining out that day. It may not surprise you that people seeking restaurants were eager to eat out, but similar results came through for auto and
travel industries as well. Forty-nine percent of auto searchers and 33%
of travel searches planned to purchase within twenty-four hours. Mobile
customers are motivated and eager to act.

Not only has the possibility of shopping from a mobile phone opened
up new channels of commerce, constant connectivity has altered the way
people approach shopping in brick and mortar retail stores as well. We've
become used to having access to information as close as our pockets at

all times. Customers are using their smartphones both to make purchases and to inform shopping decisions. More than half of the people with smartphones used their phone while in a store to research products and compare prices. Savvy consumers are searching the internet to make sure they're getting the best deals and the products that best meet their needs.

When surveyed, 53% of consumers who decided not to purchase an item in a store did so after consulting their mobile device. Of these, 38% found a better price in another store and 30% found a better price online (Source: Interactive Advertising Bureau, 2012).

These statistics may seem alarming if you're a brick and mortar retailer who doesn't want your store to be used as a showroom. But there are some exciting opportunities for all retailers relating to these statistics and our emerging shopping habits. The mobile device can offer a complete shopping experience to your customers or can be part of a blend of traditional brick and mortar business, online shopping experience, and convenient mobile commerce platform. Retailers can't ignore the 66% of US smartphone users who report using their mobile device to inform shopping decisions (Source: Leo J. Shapiro and Associates, 2012).

Once you understand how your customers interact with their mobile devices, you can create shopping opportunities for them that meet their needs and close sales.

Mobile provides the possibility of additional opportunities to engage with customers. Offering a mobile optimized website can raise engagement and the likelihood of customers to interact with your brand on their mobile devices by as much as eighty-five percent. By making every interaction with customers as easy on them as possible and engaging them where they are, brands can optimally position themselves. Building a mobile optimized shopping experience is a relevant way to serve your customers and reach a broader audience.

For retailers, it's important to understand how your customers relate to mobile and utilize their mobile devices to inform and complete shopping decisions. Marketing strategies should take into account mobile customer preferences and habits in order to not lose sales to other retailers. Convenience and ease of use is key.

15. Mobile Commerce

□ □ □

There's another side to this of course. Savvy retailers can expand their customer base by offering meaningful mobile commerce opportunities.

Creating a mobile commerce site and app can both help you attract new customers and increase your exposure to existing customers. We already know that people are always connected and that they tend to be action-oriented when using mobile devices. As a retailer, being available when they are and at the time of decision can make all the difference. Mobile customers tend to know what they are looking for and are quick to make purchasing decisions.

The development costs for mobile commerce sites are reasonable. With internet based software and services, you can create a customized mobile commerce site easily and quickly with no expertise. The same is possible for apps. As you may know, my company Launch & Hustle offers custom mobile apps (iOS & Android) for small businesses for as low as $68/mo and can have your app in the App Store and Google Play in less than a month. There's no excuses left for not having your own mobile app and truly being in the palm of your customer's hand.

Check out some mobile commerce sites and apps and notice the features they highlight. Mobile stores are generally much less complicated than desktop digital retail sites. When you're shopping on your mobile, pay attention to what works and what doesn't. Is the process quick and simple? How did you feel during the after the purchase? Take notes, ask family and friends their opinions and learn from what people are telling you. You can avoid a lot of costly mistakes by simply asking a few questions up front.

Remember, there is less space on mobile. Some of your customers will be using tablets, which gives them a bit more room, but you have to count on most transactions occurring on screens no bigger than a deck of cards. It's important to edit information and decrease clutter so that shoppers can focus on the products, prices, and CTA. Product pages need to have all the essential information and *only* the essential information. Edit out any unnecessary elements and give them an option to click for more info.

Focus on the elements that will inform a decision to make a purchase and make sure the price is clearly displayed. Other important elements to feature are a product description, add-to-cart button, and any delivery charges. You would be smart to add customer reviews and a button to share on social media as well.

Customer service is important and offering customers easy ways to reach you on their mobile devices and from your mobile commerce site makes sense. Click to call, email buttons, or even Skype chat should be included. If you have a brick and mortar store, the site can direct customers to the nearest location using GPS services.

As with all mobile development, keep the site simple, quick and easy to read. Buttons must be clear and large for easy navigation.

In order to maximize conversion, the checkout process should be seamless and simple. Ask for minimum checkout information. Forms should be as brief as possible and if returning customers have pre-registered, let them use their preferred settings for abbreviated checkout. Registration should not be compulsory. The goal should be to enable the customer to complete a purchase with as few steps as possible. Checkout can be a standard credit or debit card checkout, or use a payment system such as PayPal. Using a payment system simplifies the process for people who prefer this method of payment and offers additional security to consumers.

Once you have built your site and app, you'll be able to test them. Learn from what's working and what isn't, and adjust to meet your customer's needs and increase sales. As with everything on mobile, all customer interactions are trackable.

☐ ☐ ☐

16. Mobile Email

I know this has happened to you: You receive an email on your mobile device and try to open it but can't make sense of it because of a wide format, small font, or slow-loading features. There might be a link to click that takes you to a site that isn't mobile optimized and you get frustrated and pledge to return to that email later, leaving it in your inbox only until you forget about it or eventually delete it when you're tidying up your inbox.

You're not alone. Remember, we tend to want interactions to be quick and meaningful on mobile. And it's pretty likely that just like you, your customers are opening the emails you send them from their mobile devices and plan on giving your message about ten seconds of their time. Are you making that time count?

One of the most used functions on mobile devices is email. According to a Portia research survey in 2012, 669.5 million people used mobile email in 2011; by 2016 this is expected to grow to 2.4 billion. In a spare moment people tend to first check their email. It's the way they stay connected and fill what might otherwise be wasted time. As you might expect, people who open email on a mobile device read and respond to the message very quickly.

We talked about customer personas. How often are your personas actually sitting at their desks waiting for you to reach out to them? Exactly.

□ □ □

You've got permission, you're creating and sharing relevant content, but that's all meaningless if it's complicated, hard to read, and slow to load.

Because so many people will open the email that you send with their mobile devices, it makes sense to optimize email for mobile. Out of respect for your customers and their time, keep mobile-optimized email copy brief and to the point. In truth, that's good practice for desktop email as well. And since you don't have any control over where your customers will be when they receive your message, you might as well optimize for mobile and a positive experience for your customers.

Get your point across with clarity of purpose. People tend to skim on mobile. We tend to skim, in general. Our attention spans are abbreviated and this is even more the case when we use mobile devices.

When creating email that is optimized for mobile, consider including:

▷ A CTA: Coupons, deals, promotions, and special offers.

▷ Compelling and relevant content.

▷ Helpful information. Typically with a link to expanded info.

There should be a reason you reached out to the customer. Email is not evergreen, and in theory people can open email messages whenever they choose. In reality, we scroll through our email messages in spare moments. Be certain your message is timely, relevant, and offers value.

Email messages require a clear CTA. Don't be afraid to ask customers directly. State the CTA twice, once near the beginning and again closer to the end. That way, customers who don't want to read everything can quickly act, and those who read to the end aren't forced to skim back over the content to remember what you wanted them to do. Make the CTA stand out and hyperlink it if possible. Make it easy for the reader to transition from the email to the next step. The CTA or response should be optimized for mobile too, and should ask for a simple and brief action. Expect your customers to be able to read the email and complete the CTA in less than thirty seconds. If they want more information, provide links to a site where they can get more in-depth, but in the email itself, respect their time and increase your chances of getting the response you want.

▷ Subject lines should be action-oriented, relevant, compelling and brief (five to seven words).

▷ Because screens are small, text should be large.

▷ Choose a simple and easy to read font. Elegant cursives and fancy serif fonts don't translate well to the small screen.

▷ A mobile-optimized email should have minimal vertical scrolling and no horizontal scrolling or pinching.

▷ Encourage sharing. Let them know they can pass the message on to their friends.

▷ Consider including a plain text version. You never know when your reader will be in a bad cellular zone and have trouble loading images.

▷ Make sure that all the important aspects of your message are still visible if reader chooses to view without images.

▷ Links should be clickable and obvious.

▷ Be sure your "from line" is descriptive. For smaller businesses a person's name (could be in combination with your business name) feels more personal to your customers and can produce better open rates.

▷ Offer compelling content and positive offers that will make your customers happy to open the next message from you.

IMPERATIVE

▷ Remember that each interaction is part of the customer's path and needs to leave a positive impression.

▷ If you don't have anything important to say, wait until you do.

▷ Your email should be relevant and offer value to the customer.

▷ Always have a link for customers to change their permission settings.

The best test is this: How would you feel if you received your message? Does it seem intrusive, pushy, or difficult to decipher? Or is it casual, friendly, and respectful of your prospect's valuable time? Nowadays every mobile user expects to receive promotional messages; make sure yours are welcome.

□ □ □

17. Mobile Ad Networks

Mobile ad networks offer highly targetable advertising options. Mobile ads can be hyperlocal and targeted to individuals in specific locations and with designated search preferences.

Mobile ad placement can be controlled by info like zip codes, neighborhoods, as well as GPS location.

As consumers continue to use smartphones and mobile apps to make decisions, plan their afternoon, choose a restaurant and decide which stores to frequent, they are likely to act on businesses that are geographically close to them. With mobile advertising, local marketers like to apply an 80-20 rule. Eighty percent of business will come from the closest twenty percent of users. People tend to visit local businesses when they within a short walk or drive.

The local and proximity features aren't only useful for Main Street brick and mortar businesses, though. People are defined by their environments, and targeting a specific market with products or services that are relevant and appealing to them makes sense.

Advertising on mobile phones can be rewarding and easy to manage. Google mobile ads, AdMob, InMobi, Mojiva and Millennial Media offer options that are easy to implement yourself. You can choose the platforms you wish to advertise on and create your own ad. Mobile adverting can be targeted by age, gender, location, interests, recent searches, and many other factors. These ads work on a cost-per-click basis and you can set a limit on the amount that you want to spend. Your campaign will be easy to track and you'll be able to determine the ROI on the ads fairly quickly. As with any mobile marketing campaign, it's essential to be sure that when someone responds, they are directed to an app, site or page that is mobile friendly.

□ □ □

18. Mobile Websites

Mobile users expect instant information. Whether they're entertaining themselves while waiting for an appointment, quickly checking email, or searching for a solution, the time a customer devotes to mobile per session tends to be abbreviated.

Don't alienate your customer! Respect their time by creating solutions that load quickly and are simple to navigate. When faced with a bad mobile experience:

▷ 62% will abandon website and seek alternative brands.

▷ 20% will complete their transaction but will never return.

▷ 10% will abandon and return later via computer.

When designing for mobile, simplicity is essential. Complicated menus and multiple navigational features will make navigation more challenging.

The small screen size of mobile devices necessitates an adapted plan of action. Simplified graphics are essential, as is clear and targeted content. Buttons and navigational features should be clearly identifiable and easy to utilize. Nothing can be complicated. Text must be large enough to be legible and it's important that links aren't too close to each other and are optimized for simple touch screen navigation. Remember that the total screen space of a mobile device ranges from a few inches tall to the size of a paperback book, and that users are often multi-tasking or rushing when engaging with mobile devices.

Every aspect of your mobile plan needs to consider speed, simplicity, and size.

Site features should be edited for mobile. While a customer might linger and explore additional features and details of a traditional website, they are more task-driven when using mobile devices. When creating a mobile site, it's essential to have a clear, well thought-out strategy. Imagine your customer's experience and anticipate their needs. Time your site. Does it take longer than two seconds to load on a mobile phone? Aim to have all features loaded and functioning in less than two seconds. If your site exceeds this, simplify!

Benchmark your campaign against others that are effective. Check out mobile websites of successful companies from your own mobile device. Pay attention to what works and what doesn't. Amazon's mobile site is very simple. The landing page is basically a single search box. Netflix's mobile website is basically a search for streaming movies and shows.

Your existing site can help you make some choices of what to feature on a mobile landing page. Use analytics to determine the most common uses of your site. This will help you determine what information and features should be highlighted. If most customers who access your site from a mobile device want to know store hours, make sure that they are prominent and easy to find.

Most mobile sites don't have as many pages as desktop sites do. Mobile users are looking for the most salient information as quickly as possible. Some mobile sites offer a feature that allows users to go to the regular site if they wish. This is a good idea if you've really simplified your site to meet the needs of your mobile audience. Netflix's mobile site is great, for example, if you want to stream a movie. But if you were hoping to add a DVD to your queue, you're out of luck.

18. MOBILE WEBSITES

□ □ □

Small screen size needs to be considered when editing features as well as arranging them.

The site must be able to be viewed on a pocket-sized device by someone who is likely to be distracted. Make it as easy as you can on your customers by editing your site for simplicity.

On a mobile site it's important that the search features be customizable by the customer in order to narrow search results. Let customers choose the number of results to show, so that they don't become overwhelmed. It's also a good idea to let them choose to sort search results by price (ascending and descending), most popular, or availability. If your customers can find what they're looking for quickly and accurately, they are more likely to act and to return.

An empty search is a missed opportunity, especially if you're selling products. If the original search term isn't found, you may want to have the search make suggestions for your customers, as people tend to make quick decisions on mobile devices and you don't want them to leave your site feeling that their needs weren't met. Account for common misspellings to anticipate the desires of your customers or have recommended searches prepopulate as your customer types, such as on Google.

Make prices clear and easy to find on mobile. Customers tend to use their mobile devices for comparison-shopping. Make shopping easy by displaying prices prominently. As mobile customers tend to act quickly, it's also a good idea to have a simple and secure checkout feature on the same screen as the product.

As your site needs to be easy to navigate and read for mobile users with all different devices, keeping the features and design simple makes it easier to translate to more platforms.

Remember, it wasn't long ago that mobile devices had limited color options and four-way navigational buttons. But keeping a site simple enough to easily load and navigate is more valuable than having complicated features that will confuse users and delay loading. Less is more.

IMPERATIVE

□ □ □

√ *INTERACTIVE MOBILE WEBSITE EXPLORATION OPPORTUNITY*

For an example of some mobile sites that are designed with customer ease in mind check out:

WholeFoods.com

Amazon.com

□ □ □

19. Location

Location is a not to be a missed opportunity for mobile marketing. While mobile marketing can be global, it can also be hyper-local. There are moments when a mobile customer is at a specific location where a company can offer value. They can provide helpful and relevant information to customers both in the moment and specific to where they are in the world. Even if a customer isn't in the position to make a purchase right then, it's still important to reach out. A customer can check-in via an app that will track their location, and they can learn about real estate that is available in the area or restaurants and businesses that might meet their needs based on their demographic and preferences. You can also use geo fencing to automatically send push notifications to customers who have your mobile app and are within a certain proximity to your business. More on this in the mobile apps section.

If a customer has already interacted with your brand, you can better serve them by offering them information relevant to their geographical location such as local branch locations.

While location is important to all businesses, local businesses and those with physical brick and mortar stores can really benefit from location services. There was a time when the internet changed the face of retail to the extent that having a physical store seemed irrelevant. The expense of physical stores and their associated overhead became a liability. But mobile has changed this. Not only can you help customers find the best deals by comparative shopping options right in their own neighborhoods, but mobile helps establish a sense of community and immediacy for local businesses. Local businesses and businesses with physical locations have learned to make the experience of coming into their space a positive and important part of doing business. Mobile is transforming these brick and mortar businesses again by reaching out to local customers and letting them know how they can benefit from being part of the in-store culture. While we are part of the global community, we are also very much connected to our neighborhoods and the necessities and pleasures of everyday life.

Sure, you can order a book from Amazon, but if you know your local bookstore is having a reading by a favorite novelist, might you venture out to meet her and have an enriching experience? If your gourmet market is having a tasting or cooking demonstration, customers might enjoy and appreciate the opportunity to interact with neighbors and taste the offerings of the market. In my neighborhood, there's a little wine shop that has tastings every evening from six until seven. They've been doing this for a few months. During the first few weeks there were only a few participants, but as word spread through mobile email, social media, and text, the gatherings grew. They made their messages simple, easy to share, and inviting. It's become a perfect place for many to stop in after work and try the featured beverages and socialize for a few minutes. Yes, you can order wine online. But can you taste it alongside your neighbors? The local wine shop is using mobile and new media marketing to cultivate a following and to grow their client base, you should too.

Using research about your customers along with mobile location services is a great way to fine-tune your message. If you learn that your customers have certain preferences and habits, you can better meet their needs. Consider information from your customers as well as geographic information such as season and weather. Is there a big game in their hometown? A marathon? Is it snowing or exceptionally hot? Are the kids on a break from school? How might these factors and more influence your customers and what can you do to make their lives easier?

19. Location

□ □ □

In some areas, grocery stores have taken local to the extreme. Shoppers are able to use their smartphone to scan the groceries as they put them in the cart. As they walk through the aisles, coupons and discounts flash onto the phone's screen. It knows that they're in the dairy aisle and may point out a special offer on yogurt that is only available to smartphone users. At the checkout shoppers can scan the phone at the register to pay.

The grocery store is able to use customer data to refine buying and marketing decisions as well as to push certain items that may be relevant and specific to the customer's location as well as purchase history. They may even learn ways to change the layout of the store based on the paths that customers tend to take while shopping. Your business may not be ready to offer self-scan and pay options yet, but the opportunities for location-based mobile marketing are vast and growing. Be willing to experiment now and employ location-based strategies to your mobile campaigns as well and think ahead to ways you might reach customers in the future.

Have fun with it!

□ □ □

20. Mobile Apps

When developing a mobile strategy, a marketing manager – whether he or she works for a multinational conglomerate or a regional small business – is faced with wide array of choices. Nowhere is this more apparent than in the rapidly expanding market of mobile apps. As of January 2014, mobile apps overtook PC internet usage in the U.S. According to comScore, Mobile devices accounted for 55% of Internet usage in the United States in January 2014. Apps made up 47% of Internet traffic and 8% of traffic came from mobile browsers. PCs weighted in at 45%.

> **Mobile devices accounted for 55% of Internet usage in the United States in January 2014.**

As of this writing more than a 1.5 million apps are available for sale or download through the App Store and Google Play alone, according to Canalys, but there are a lot more app stores than this, including Windows Phone Marketplace, and BlackBerry App World. If you go online and search for mobile app developers, you'll find dozens of companies that will design and build an app for your company. You tell the designer the functions that you want and the market you're trying to reach, and soon, or not so soon in some cases, your company can have its very own app that your customers can use on their smartphones.

But we're getting ahead of ourselves. When reading about apps, more than one business owner or marketing manager will scratch his or her head and think, "Okay – but what's an app? What do they do and how can it benefit my business?"

THE WORLD OF MOBILE APPS

Mobile applications (apps) are specialized software programs that are embedded into hand-held communication devices such as mobile phones, tablet computers, personal digital assistants (PDAs) or gaming consoles.

For a business, a mobile app should solve a problem either for the business or for the customer. An example of an app that helps a business is one used by a sales rep on their smartphone to submit orders from the field. These are internal apps that the public doesn't see.

In this book we'll focus on apps that are designed to strengthen your marketing effort, and are used by your customers. Mobile apps can provide a wide range of services to your customers; add tremendous value (such as apps that enhance customer relationships or experiences). You can provide front line customer service with social media integration, drive in store sales with push notifications or geo fencing, build customer loyalty with reward programs or make money with ecommerce. In the retail sector, mobile apps can help customers look up product information, see photos and videos, read product reviews, search for local stores, access daily deals and discounts, contact customer service, make secure purchases from their mobile devices, and share information and products they find relevant and interesting to their network.

> **Mobile apps can provide a wide range of services to your customers**

Developing and offering an app can allow your business to offer deals, provide updates, share services, or connect with customers. A restaurant could develop an app that alerts customers of lunch or dinner specials via push notification, has a built in loyalty program, gives them easy access to their menu, the ability to make reservations or order takeout, and leave positive reviews. A business coach app could have video tutorials and podcasts available to prospects, client only areas with special content, lead capture pages, a click to call feature, or the ability for clients to schedule their next appointment. A real estate agent could develop an app that features their listings, offers home-buying tips, automatically sends out push notifications to buyers within a certain proximity to their open house, and integrates social sharing. The options are endless and can be applied to virtually any business type for an excellent ROI.

PLAN YOUR APP STRATEGY

Faced with a huge number of choices, like any other business strategy, using mobile apps requires careful planning. Consider:

▷ Your marketing goal.

▷ Whom you are targeting.

▷ What you want your target audience to do.

▷ Who is responsible for making it happen?

▷ How you will evaluate its effectiveness.

Developing a simple action plan is a good way to be clear about why and how you would use mobile apps. Here are some key points to remember.

✓ Think about the features you need on your app. Do you want to make sales, get customer feedback, or deepen your customers' connection with your brand by engaging them in a way that has nothing to do with sales? Are any of these components already available? Perhaps you have existing material or expertise that you could use as the basis for an app. For example, have you written content for your website that you could easily convert into app form, or programs for your customers or staff?

✓ Think about what you already know or do that could work as an app. For example, a restaurant might develop an app that lets customers learn about wines and pair them with entrée selections.

✓ An app can only reach people with a mobile device with which it's compatible. You need to consider whether your target market's profile fits with the smartphone or tablet user profile, or both. Then you need to consider which platform they use (iPhone, Android, BlackBerry, etc.). Apps may need to be adapted separately for each of the mobile platforms. You need to carefully consider which device or devices fit the profile of your target market so that your customers can use your app.

✓ Mobile apps work best when they're used as part of a larger marketing campaign, which may include social media and other marketing channels. Cross channel marketing is an important aspect of every marketing strategy and a great way to expand the reach and adoption of your app.

✓ To be effective an app has to be used by your customers. If you want them to use it, you need to tell them about it. An app cannot sell itself. To bring it to the attention of the marketplace your app may require its own marketing campaign. You will need a plan to get your app to its target audience. Suggestions include making sure all your other marketing tools, including your website and social media presence, invite people to download your app. Promote your app widely in all your marketing and customer contacts, both in store and online.

✓ Make sure your app delivers value to the person who has taken the time to download and use it. Every interaction needs to be meaningful and add value to the overall brand experience while drawing the customer closer to your brand. When people use your app for the first time, they should intuitively grasp the most important features. Don't waste the opportunity to delight, to wow, and to make life easier for your customer.

✓ Track your mobile app results. It's worthwhile to monitor the impact of your mobile apps on your business, so you know what works and what doesn't. Seeing how many people download your app is of some value, but it's much more meaningful to track things like frequency of use and outcomes like sales or other conversions. In fact, Apple's app-store-ranking algorithm seems to have recently changed. It used to be that apps that were most downloaded ranked highest, but now there is an increased emphases on active usage instead. Using a website analytics tool, you may be able to measure visits to your website that are generated by an app. Integrating coupons, promotion codes or a loyalty program into your app my help you track sales generated from it as well.

Push notifications have many of the same elements as text messages. Customers set up preferences on an application and allow push notifications to be sent to them. Notifications are instantly delivered to a smartphone and are displayed on the screen and many customers have set up their preferences to have an auditory reminder when a push notification comes through.

Push notifications are very similar to traditional text. If you have opted in to receive push notifications from Groupon for deals in your area, notifications will arrive daily. If an offer appeals to you, purchasing is simple: click or slide the icon to be directed to the app from which you can purchase the product or gift certificate immediately. As the customer's payment information and shipping address is already stored, the checkout process is seamless. The ability to act instantly relates well to the habits of mobile users and makes it easy for them to complete a task.

Push notifications are a great option for one-to-many communications and for the delivery of timely and actionable information. In the case of the Groupon daily push, customers receive an option to purchase from a selection of a few daily specials. Their choice is binary: purchase or disregard. But there's no reason why push notification can't direct customers to a place where they have more agency or opportunities to interact. Ultimately, push notifications are preferred over SMS (text messages) for one-to-many communications because they are free. Businesses who have a mobile app can benefit from this ongoing savings as well as the customer loyalty and branding benefits that come along with having their app on a device that their customer is looking at continuously throughout the day.

Not all mobile devices can receive push notifications. While the ability to send and receive SMS messages is nearly ubiquitous on hand-held mobile devices, only smartphones can receive push notifications. With most cell phone plans replacing mobile devices for customers every two years, the turnover rate for outdated hardware is fairly quick. It won't be long before virtually all devices support applications and therefore push notifications. Your target customer is probably already there.

The original cost of setting up an app may be higher than SMS, but once the delivery system is established there is no cost per message and there are plenty of other benefits as well.

In order to establish a push campaign, you must have an app. I personally prefer mobile apps and push notifications over SMS for businesses looking to engage customers and drive action because of their reduced long term costs, branding power, commerce options, and customer loyalty benefits. Not to mention that app use is the most popular among consumers. SMS certainly has its place and the simplicity, ease of use for both businesses and customers, and its extremely high adoption make it a worthwhile option as well. I use both for my business and love the flexibility, ability to experiment, and insights I gain. We'll discuss SMS more thoroughly in a later chapter, but your decision will come down to your goals and what fits best for your business model

> **I personally prefer mobile apps and push notifications over SMS for businesses looking to engage customers**

At the end of the day your customers want to feel smart and empowered when they use your app. If something goes wrong, give clear recovery instructions but don't burden them with the technical details. People of all ages and cultures should feel firmly in control and never overwhelmed by too many choices or irrelevant flash. If you make your app fun, easy to use, and useful, then the profits will take care of themselves.

21. Augmented Reality

One of the latest buzzwords in mobile marketing is "augmented reality." No, it's not something that happens to you at Burning Man when you eat something strange given to you by your friend. In the world of mobile communications, augmented reality (AR) is a view of a physical, real-world environment whose elements are augmented by computer-generated sensory input such as sound, video, graphics or GPS data. Graphical augmentation is presented in real time and is linked with environmental elements. With the help of advanced AR technology, the information about the scene presented on the mobile screen can become interactive.

An early and very simple version of augmented reality was introduced back in the 1980s in the cockpits of fighter jets, where real-time flight information was projected directly onto the pilot's windscreen. The pilot saw the actual landscape in front of him, but without taking his eyes away from the windscreen he also saw graphical elements that told him his speed, altitude, and other information. Today, thanks to computer miniaturization, these capabilities, and much more, are available for handheld devices.

The necessary hardware components for augmented reality include a processor, display, sensors, and input devices. Modern mobile computing devices like smartphones and tablet computers contain these elements, which often include a camera and MEMS sensors such as accelerometer,

□ □ □

GPS, and solid state compass, making them suitable AR platforms. The display of information can be accomplished by various technologies including optical projection systems, monitors, hand held devices, and display systems worn on one's person.

For business and commerce, augmented reality has many applications. AR can be used as an aid in selecting products from a catalog or through a kiosk. AR can enhance product previews such as allowing a customer to view what's inside a product's packaging without opening it. Scanned images of products can activate views of additional content such as customization options and additional images of the product in use. AR can also be used to integrate print and video marketing. Printed marketing material can be designed with certain "trigger" images that, when scanned by an AR enabled device using image recognition, activate a video version of the promotional material and offering users an enhanced experience.

EXAMPLES OF AR MOBILE APPLICATIONS

Here are some examples of existing AR apps for mobile devices. There are hundreds, and like regular mobile apps, they can be custom-designed to fit your marketing strategy and goals.

▷ The Golfscape GPS Rangefinder is an augmented reality range finder for golfers. Loaded into the app's memory is data from over 35,000 golf courses. Hold your phone up to your shot and it displays the distance from front, center, and back of green.

▷ New York Nearest Subway shows you all thirty-three lines of the New York subway system, displayed in colored arrows. By tilting the phone upwards, you see the nearest stations, what direction they are in relation to your location, how many miles away they are, and what lines they are on. If you continue to tilt the phone upwards, you see stations further away, as stacked icons.

▷ DanKam for iPhone is an augmented reality application for those who are suffering from color-blindness. DanKam "sees" colors — and the differences between colors — and alters them so they're more visible to the color blind.

▷ SpyGlass gives you additional information about the landscape you're in. It features a hi-tech viewfinder, milspec compass, gyrocompass, maps, GPS tracker, speedometer, optical rangefinder, visual sextant, gyro horizon, inclinometer, angular calculator, 5x zoom sniper scope, and camera. You can find and track your position, identify multiple locations, get your bearings, and locate the sun, the moon, and stars, all in real time.

▷ Theodolite is a multi-function augmented reality app that combines a compass, GPS, map, photo/movie camera, rangefinder, and two-axis inclinometer. Theodolite overlays real time information about position, altitude, bearing, range, and inclination on the iPhone's live camera image, like an electronic viewfinder.

▷ Panoramascope computes the skyline of the landscape visible from your current location and shows it on top of the iPhone's camera view. Peaks and other points of interest are labeled, and the app gives you information about your surroundings. If you're a couch potato, you can also select a viewpoint by searching from hundreds of thousands of placenames.

▷ 3D Compass (AR Compass) is a compass app with augmented reality view and real time map update, and provides real time location information. Basically, the key element is a graphical representation of a one of those dashboard ball compasses that turns as you turn. It's useful for travel, camping, and outdoor activities.

▷ Robotvision is an augmented reality application for iPhone that lets you explore your surroundings more effectively. It uses the iPhone accelerometer, compass, and other OS features to find stores and other listings around you, using the data feeds from Bing.com, making it the first iPhone app to incorporate Bing on an iPhone.

▷ For the bicycle enthusiast, Cyclepedia features over one hundred iconic bicycles. It lets you zoom, pan, and rotate them 360°. With a polished interface it shows origin, specs, and details, and it also features films, original advertising, links, engineering drawings, and still photos.

▷ Layar Reality Browser displays digital "layers" on your smartphone's camera view, enhancing your view of the real world. Links and videos help you interact with and learn more about objects and locations in your field of vision. You can point, scan, and view objects enhanced with Layar, such as newspapers, magazines, and ads, to see links and other digital extras appear on top of the content you view every day.

How AR can work for you

The common thread of all of these augmented reality apps is that they take the information received by the phone's camera – generally the scene that you see in front of you – and layer on additional information in the form of text or graphical elements. This additional information comes from static databases (for example, the address of the restaurant you see on the screen) and from dynamic real-time sources (for example, the location of the moving subway train relative to your subway station). They also can trigger the phone to go to another URL or play a video (for example, when you point your phone at a magazine ad with AR built in, the graphic on the ad tells the phone to play a video that makes the page come to life and provides additional info to the consumer).

A simple form of augmented reality is a Quick Response code, those black-and-white squares that look like glorified bar codes. When you point your phone at the QR code, it instructs your phone to show you a website that is related to the entity on which the QR code was printed. In the following chapter I'll discuss QR codes in more detail.

The possibilities for mobile marketing are endless. You can create an augmented reality app for your business that will enhance your customers' experiences, give them valuable product information, tell them what's on sale, let them see an item in different colors, or even show them where to park their car. It's a powerful tool that can entertain, inform, and bring your customer closer to your brand.

22. QR Codes

Y ou've seen them on advertisements, real estate signs, and in the newspaper – those square boxes that look like jumbled bar codes. They're quick response (QR) codes.

QR codes are basically hyperlinks printed on paper or another surface that create a bridge between the physical world and the virtual world. Customers scan a QR code with the camera of a smartphone or tablet, and the screen of the device shows a mobile landing page, video or other form of media. The possibilities are almost endless.

QR codes generally contain about 350 times as much information as a traditional one-dimensional bar code. They were invented in Japan by Denso Wave (a division of Toyota) to be used in the automotive industry. But in Japan, QR codes quickly became part of every day life.

If you look in your refrigerator, it's likely you have some QR codes on the packaging of your orange juice or yogurt. You'll find them printed in magazine advertisements and on posters at local stores. They are present in outdoor advertising on city streets, subway platforms, bus stops and billboards. QR codes are showing up in some strange places too; there are QR codes on taxis, buses and trucks. Have you tried to scan a moving vehicle?

IMPERATIVE

□ □ □

WHY QR?

QR codes act as a link between print media and the web. One of the main problems with traditional print advertising is that there is no way to understand its influence. You can't track impressions when customers look through magazines or come across a sign. You have to wait to see if sales improve to gauge a campaign's success. And even then, it's challenging to weed out other influences. QR codes allow people to take the next step in connecting with your brand. After encountering a print ad, product packaging, or in-store sign with a QR code, if a customer chooses to scan the code, you'll be able to collect some valuable data and at the same time have another opportunity to serve your customer.

As of June 2011, more than 30% of US adults have a QR code reader app on their mobile device. (Source: Prosper Mobile Insights, June 2011). In 2011, overall QR code scans increased 300% over 2010 (ScanLife).

With a little education and some incentive, customers seem to be willing to give scanning QR codes a try. We just need to make it worth their while. First of all, they are free. It doesn't cost anything to create a QR code, and you have the opportunity to offer your customers more information or a richer experience as they engage with your brand. QR codes are easy to track, as they direct the user to a landing page for which you can set up analytics to measure response. QR codes are not device specific and neither are the landing pages they link to.

QR codes offer an opportunity to create engaging and useful content that a user can access directly from a mobile device. It's a way to cross-channel from print to digital.

While you can't quickly change the printed material with the QR codes on them, you can alter the landing page they are directed to. So if customers are scanning your QR code but they're not taking the next step in engaging, you can swiftly and inexpensively adjust the message you're giving them.

Like all digital marketing strategies, QR Codes have minimal environmental impact and can make printed material more efficient by eliminating waste. If hefty instruction manuals that come with products were simply QR codes printed on a tiny sticker, imagine all the paper we would save.

WHERE DO QR CODES TAKE THE USER?

The most common destinations of QR codes are videos, social media, e-commerce, and data-capture.

More than half of all QR codes in magazines in 2011 led to a video (54%). Video content can include a product demonstration, more information about a product, or even some amusing or entertaining content that would appeal to the customers. Don't miss the opportunity to delight. With a QR code, you can even simply direct customers to videos on YouTube.

Fifty-three percent of US smartphone users who have used a QR code did so to get a coupon, discount or deal (Source: MGH, via MediaPost, April 2011). QR codes are useful for coupons, as each can have identifying data.

Data-capture pages are often contests or loyalty programs where customers are asked to opt-in for future communication.

Some QR codes lead to social media pages, and others led to stores where products can be purchased instantly.

In subway stations in Korea, Tesco Home Plus, a supermarket chain, installed signs with printed images of life-sized supermarket shelves stocked with photos of popular products. While waiting for their train, commuters are able to scan the QR code below the products they would like to purchase and have them delivered directly to their homes. Consumers appreciate the convenience of using their commute time to complete a necessary task. And Tesco has been able to increase sales without building more stores.

For companies, QR codes are alluring because they're easy to create, they don't cost much to implement, and they can be easily tracked. They also offer endless opportunities to interact with your customers.

Imperative

□ □ □

For customers, however, QR codes can be confusing. You're asking them to take their phone out of their pocket, open the scanning app (assuming they already have one), line up the code, and scan. It's not as quick as it sounds. So, while it may be faster than typing in a URL, if you're asking the consumer to take action, the destination must be worth the effort.

Printed QR codes often don't indicate what the pay-off is for the effort the customer has to exert in order to interact. While customers are likely to be curious about where a QR code will lead, it's a good idea to give them some information about its ultimate destination. If there is a contest, let them know. Make sure the customer has some indication of what to expect.

All QR codes are designed to be scanned by mobile devices. So, 100% of QR code landing pages need to be mobile optimized. There is no excuse for directing a customer from a QR code to a landing page that isn't mobile friendly.

Consider the context. The QR code should either offer additional information or entertain (or both) and should be directly related to the printed material scanned.

QR codes can store up to 7,089 numbers and a variety of data including text, website links, telephone numbers, email, contact details (vCard), calendar events (vCalendar), and hyperlinks to photos, videos, app downloads, social media pages, map directions, and more.

CHANNEL MARKETING

In telecommunications, a channel is a discreet path through which signals can flow. On the web, a channel is a preselected URL that sends information for immediate viewing upon request; and in digital marketing, a channel is a "middleman" between the message creator and the user or audience. QR codes create a new channel of communication from a passive medium, such as print ads, business cards or other marketing swag, to a user's smartphone device.

Marketers love them because they offer an inexpensive and effortless channel to connect users to their websites and/or other advertisements, while many users hate them because of the less-than-stellar experience. Unfortunately, QR codes have gotten a bad rap because this channel of communications has been abused at the hands of inexperienced marketers. I'm not saying all marketers abuse them, but I think it's fair to say that everyone reading this has taken the time to pull out your mobile phone, download an app, and scan a QR code, only to be taken to a regular website (pinch-n-pull), or even worse a website designed in Flash, which isn't even recognized by most smartphone browsers. Don't be that guy!

Consider places that might work to use QR codes in your own business be sure that each code has text near to it that indicates the pay-off for the customer. Be creative. Customers can use QR codes to get more information such as assembly instructions, video tutorials, and in-depth or insider content that wouldn't fit on packaging or printed material. Or QR codes can be a quick way for customers to scan products they wish to purchase. You can also design a scavenger hunt or similar games for customers around your business or community. The point is, be creative and find fun ways for people to engage, get informed and be entertained.

✓ *For an example QR code for you to scan see the back cover of this book.*

☐ ☐ ☐

23. SMS

We've become accustomed to using text for the exchange of quick information, and we expect recipients to glance at message promptly. We're used to looking at text messages as soon as they come in. We have trained ourselves to pay attention to text and most of us have set an auditory alert to indicate the arrival of a text message. When someone is running late for a meeting, we appreciate it if they let us know with a quick text. And we're able to reply quickly and simply with a return text.

Short message service (SMS) is one of the easiest and simplest features on a mobile device. SMS is an instant disruption. Texts are instant and are generally more urgent than email. They are brief and should be meaningful.

Digital communication such as texting has become so integrated into our culture that we've adopted a shorthand language. Abbreviations like LOL and OMG have even found their way into dictionaries such as *The Oxford English Dictionary*.

Text messages only come through when the phone is on and when you're in an active cell network. (And what we already know about mobile usage, is this is almost always.) If a mobile device is turned off or is out of a service area, as soon as it is back online, the messages are delivered and the recipient is alerted.

There are SMS text apps for devices that don't use a cellular network, such as for the iPod touch and tablets. These adapt SMS text to go over wifi networks and deliver them instantly in much the same manner as carrier delivered SMS texts messages.

SMS has an almost universal reach. Nearly all cell phones have SMS capability; from the most basic phones to the newest smartphones, text is truly platform-agnostic. Consumer pricing for receiving text messages has come down in recent years and plans have become more comprehensive with most customers opting for an unlimited text option.

Not only is text universal but customers have also indicated that they are comfortable with sending and receiving texts. It may not be the newest or sexiest feature on their phones, but it's considered to be essential. In a survey conducted by BlogHer in August of 2011, 78% of the mothers who responded report that sending and receiving text messages is the greatest benefit of their mobile phone. That means they value this feature more than the ability to make a traditional voice call.

People are already comfortable sending and receiving text messages. It's already part of their routine. As long as you respect text etiquette and keep messages time specific and useful, and you offer your customers valuable information that makes their lives and routine easier, all indications are that they would be happy to opt-in and receive pertinent text messages from you.

We tend to trust SMS text too. There is very little spam sent by text because the FCC has strict regulations for text messaging and carriers are careful to monitor and comply. That's why there is always a strict opt-in and opt-out focus on text message marketing.

As texting is instant, feedback is too. When you send out a text, you'll have the first tier of results back in a matter of minutes. Assuming your campaign had an immediate call to action, you'll not only realize the delivery rate, but the efficiency of your CTA and whether it spoke to your customers. Armed with this information, and any additional relevant factors such as redemption of coupons and purchase habits, you'll easily be able to adapt your approach to meet your customer's needs and drive more sales.

23. Sms

The real trick of an SMS campaign is finding the trigger that makes customers say, "I want that."

Sometimes all it takes is a cup of coffee. Starbucks seems to have worked this out by offering customers who enroll in the My Starbucks Rewards program a free drink on their birthdays. The program attracts coffee-loving customers with an in-store call to action. Posters and signs alert customers to the benefits of the My Starbucks Rewards program, where in addition to the free birthday beverage they can design and save their own drinks, pay with their Starbucks Card, and receive refills if they register and pay with their Starbucks Card. Starbucks offers customers a choice of opt-ins, and invites them to either visit http://www.starbucks.com/register or text the keyword "GOLD" to the short code 697289.

Starbucks then offers other layers of contact for members who have already opted-in and have established a relationship with the brand. For example, a recent Starbucks Frappuccino Happy Hour promotion offered customers half-priced frozen coffee drinks during certain afternoon hours. In order to take advantage of this deal, they provided daily SMS reminders to customers who had opted in.

Existing My Starbucks Rewards members received an email with an SMS call to action. Customers could sign up on the email or text the keyword "HAPPY" to the short code 697289. Within minutes, Starbucks texts back, "Thanks for signing up for a Frappuccino Happy Hour reminder. Reply STOP HAPPY to end, HELP HAPPY for help. Msg/data rates apply."

They have not only established another point of contact, but will be able to remind customers of the promotion in a meaningful and time-sensitive manner. Companies like Starbucks are experimenting and succeeding with SMS as a way to reward existing customers and increase loyalty.

Because consumers are already comfortable with SMS, they tend to think of it as a low-tech and simple process and are willing to engage. There isn't much of a learning curve or time commitment in sending a text. And so, in situations when immediate action is called for it can be a relevant and impactful marketing solution.

Text campaigns have proven themselves to be simple, timely, and productive, and in some cases even life changing. Following the devastating 2010 earthquake in Haiti, relief agencies and non-profits sprung into action with text-to-give campaigns and within six months raised over two billion dollars. In that same time period, the American Red Cross raised thirty-two million dollars for Haiti Earthquake relief. But, the most interesting part is that 95% of the donations that came in by text were from first-time donors.

Text works harmoniously with other media channels as well. We've already talked about the fact that Americans frequently watch two screens at once. And we know that most people keep their mobile device within arm's length at all times. Television shows like *American Idol* have integrated text into their programming and have helped to shift what would be a passive experience (watching a televised singing competition) into one in which the viewer can be an active participant. Voting for *American Idol* winners by text became so popular that the network eventually stopped breaking down the results. By the spring of 2011, season ten ended with a staggering 4.8 billion votes cast by text message.

We're quick to adopt text with brands we trust. In 2003, between the first episode of *American Idol* and the last, the number of text votes increased by almost five thousand percent.

As with any communication on a mobile device, it's essential that any links you provide direct your customers to the mobile optimized version of your content. Aim to keep all SMS text communication as brief and simple as possible. The last thing you want to do is interrupt your customer with a text that is irritating or difficult to act on. Make your message meaningful and time-specific enough to warrant a glance.

There are unlimited possibilities for adding value for your customers with SMS text messaging. Consider your customer's needs and how an instant and timely message might be useful. Go back to your customer personas and try to imagine ways that quickly reaching out to them via text might make life easier for them.

Imagine if your local auto service center sent you a text reminder when it was time for your oil change or tire rotation, and the message included a discount coupon for the service you needed. Or if your veterinarian's office sent a reminder message not only for annual check-ups and vaccinations, but sent a monthly reminder to give your dog his heart worm medication or to apply monthly flea and tick prevention. If you were a fishing enthusiast, wouldn't you appreciate it if your local bait shop sent out Saturday morning fishing updates? What if you were a busy parent and your favorite pizza shop sent out a coupon at four o'clock on a Thursday afternoon, just when you were starting to think about what to do about dinner for the kids?

Each of these examples invites immediate action. They are highly targeted, offer a valuable service to customers, and provide a chance to deepen your relationship with them.

Text messages work well for content that invites the recipient to act fast. They might mark the arrival of new merchandise that the customer has expressed an interest in and tends to sell out quickly. Text should focus on real time updates that will ultimately save customers trouble, or provide relevant information they will find useful.

▷ The hot new toy your kid was begging for just arrived.

▷ Your prescription is ready for pick-up.

▷ Tonight is your favorite networking happy hour.

▷ Soccer practice will have a one-hour rain delay.

▷ Your machine has been repaired and is ready to be picked up.

▷ You have a dentist appointment tomorrow at noon.

▷ It's time to schedule your dog's grooming.

▷ The farmer's market will have a pickling demo today at 1 pm.

▷ We have a guest chef tonight.

▷ Your cousin's band will be performing at the local pub.

▷ Your mother-in-law's plane is delayed.

▷ The wine shop is having a tasting of that whisky you were eyeing.

Messages sent by text don't have to be limited to informational blasts either. If you have permission, you can send a joke, a link to a video, or anything you think your customers will enjoy.

Keep in mind the instantaneous and urgent nature of text, though. That's the way people often reach us with a brief, "I'm running fifteen minutes behind." Or, "Save you a seat in third row, stage right." This is great, but you have to be careful to keep them engaged and to send information that is useful and meaningful enough to warrant the interruption.

When you create a text campaign it's essential to:

▷ **Know your target audience**. Understand your customers and their needs. Consider ways reaching out to them via text can make life easier for them as well as influence them.

For instance, if you own a flower shop you could drive early Valentine's Day sales and provide a simple cost effective solution by texting customers the following: *Order Valentine's Day flowers for your loved one today and receive free delivery! http://bit.ly/example or 214-555-1212*

Learn all that you can about the wants and needs of your customers, and over deliver. Be sure that your message campaign addresses their needs and exceeds their expectations. Every contact should be meaningful and positive, not intrusive.

▷ **Time interactions well.** Don't text at seven in the morning, late at night or when your customers might be in the middle of something and an interruption will be unwelcome. Be conscious about timing. The right message at the right moment can make all the difference. Be conscious of both your content and timing to achieve optimal results.

▷ **Offer something of value**. The right opt-in is essential. Often times, people use a contest as an incentive to opt-in to receive text messages from a company. A carwash might offer a drawing for a free detailing for opting in, or customers might respond better to receiving something such as a discount on their next wash. The good news is that you can experiment. A car wash that lets its best customers know when they have special offers and discounts may see an uptick in customer response. Offer an opportunity or product that will appeal to your customers. Other common examples of opt-ins are: offering timely information, polls, surveys, free offers, and daily specials. It's important to offer something of value in exchange for permission for further interaction.

▷ **Refine your message**. The content of the texts should be simple, targeted, and timely. Whatever you say must be worth that moment of interruption. Keep it brief and to the point, your customers will thank you.

▷ **Define a clear call to action.** Once your customer has read your text, he or she should have no question about what you want him or her to do. A call to action could be a coupon or discount your customer can redeem, or a link that will take them to your site or to a video with more information.

There are many possible calls to action. You can ask a survey question and then let your customers know the results at the end of the day. A bakery might text, "We're baking pies today. Which is your favorite? Text A for apple, B for blueberry." You'll be able to track the delivery rate, total # of respondents, specific answers, and more based on the system you're using. And at the same time, you can increase enthusiasm for your brand. It's important to be sure that the call to action you choose reinforces your overall marketing strategy and leads the customer closer to your brand.

▷ **Analyze success.** Don't forget to determine how you will define and track success. Have specific goals in mind and track campaigns using analytics. We'll talk more about this later, but understanding what is working and why is just as important as learning what doesn't work for you and your customers.

▷ **It's not set in stone.** The ability to easily adapt a campaign to meet the needs and preferences of your customers is one of the greatest benefits of a SMS text marketing campaign. Don't treat it as if it's a traditional, static marketing campaign and continue to do something that isn't cultivating the results you desire. Analyze and adapt. Honestly, even when things are working well, you'll want to continue to tweak things and aim for improvement.

▷ **Stay focused.** What are the specific goals of your campaign? In the end, it's likely your goals are to sell more products, influence more people, and increase your profits. We talked earlier about how to design a campaign that leads your customers one step closer to your brand with each interaction. Be sure to have clearly defined goals for each campaign you create. Don't just send out text messages because it seems like a useful or fun thing to do. In order to make progress towards your goal (any goal) it's essential to have clearly defined objectives.

- How will you alert customers to the opt-in offer and the text campaign?
- How will this integrate with other marketing campaigns and channels?

- Are messages targeted to the right customer?
- Are you giving customers the opportunity to engage by interacting?
- Does your campaign have a clear CTA?
- Are messages brief and concise?
- Is each interaction relevant and timely?

Text campaigns are a dynamic way to connect with your customers. But your first contact is not the text that you send to their mobile. How will your customers learn about you and your text campaign? Will you have signs in stores? Will the CTA be part of an email campaign? Will you use print ads? Will you spread the word with social media? All of the above? Make the CTA for text opt-in clear and easy to see in other media channels and be sure customers understand the value you are offering.

Multimedia messaging service (MMS)

Messaging can go a step further with MMS, which can include not just text, but also sound, images, and video. It is also possible (and here's where it gets really interesting from a marketer perspective) to send MMS messages from a mobile phone to an e-mail address.

According to a survey conducted in 2012 by Portia research, 207 billion MMS messages were sent in 2011, and that is expected to rise to 276.8 million in 2016 as more people become comfortable with the technology and acquire phones that support MMS.

SMS is convenient, ubiquitous, and free for those customers for whom receiving a text message is covered in their existing cell phone text-messaging plan.

The cost of setting up a SMS campaign can be as low as a penny a text for high volumes. At that rate, it's a very effective way to touch your customer with instant and actionable information. Similar to push notifications, a company can send texts to customers and get results nearly instantly.

Setting up an SMS marketing plan can be as simple as sending an email. SMS is infinitely adaptable, as you can adjust your campaigns on the fly..

STEP-BY-STEP SMS CAMPAIGN SETUP

Setting up a text campaign is really as easy as creating a blog or using any other drag and drop internet-based software.

1. Determine the groups you want to attract and their affinity. For example: Beer lovers, family dining, events, or location for multi-location restaurants.

2. Assign a short keyword to each group such as HOPS, FAMFUN, or JAZZY.

For internal purposes you can think of a keyword as the name of a specific list you're building via text. For example, HAPPY is Starbucks' list of people who joined the Frappuccino Happy Hour promotion. This tells Starbucks exactly what type of content to send to the people who opt-in to this list.

You will need to select a keyword for customers to text to the short code. With each keyword, customers can opt-in or respond to text messages. A keyword should be easy to remember and simple to type. Use the keyword to differentiate your brand. Keywords are generally not more than eight characters long. The previous example of Starbucks' Frappuccino Happy Hour promotion used the keyword HAPPY. The word "happy" has positive connotations, is relevant to the brand and specific to the promotion, is easy to remember and type, and it's sharable. Customers can remember the keyword and let their friends know how to opt-in for text reminders for 50% off frozen coffee drinks. For questions and opting out, Starbucks kept it simple and gave customers the choice of typing in STOP HAPPY (who wants to stop happy?) and HELP HAPPY.

3. You'll need a short code. Customers will need to text your keyword to a five or six digit short code (The Starbucks short code is 697289, for instance). You can either purchase a dedicated short code (expensive) for your brand or you can use a shared short code. Not surprisingly, it's less expensive to use a shared short code and is much more cost-effective for small businesses. If you have a big brand, buying your own short code might be a reasonable investment in the long run.

4. Establish a clear call to action. Your call to action must be simple and brief to increase opt-ins and make it easily sharable. Example: "Text HAPPY to 697289 for Frappuccino Happy Hour reminders." Notice that it's short, to the point and sharable on social networks like Twitter.

5. Set up your text message invitation and auto response. An invitation is sent to people you enter in the system manually to request their opt-in, and the auto response is what customers receive when initiating contact by sending the keyword to your short code. This is a great place for a special offer of some kind. For instance, "Text HOPS to 12345 and receive your first domestic draft for just $1." Or, for a live example text IMPERATIVE to 95577 to opt-in and receive my auto response.

---

for a live example text IMPERATIVE to 95577 to opt-in and receive my auto response.

---

6. Spread the word. Include your CTA in everything you do including traditional advertising, in-store signage, staff interactions with customers, and social media.

7. That's it! Once it's set up, you can begin creating and scheduling simple campaigns for each group based on their interests. Announce happy hour specials, new craft beers, photography coupons, kids eat free specials, service discounts, family nights, holiday events, new products, live music – the sky's the limit.

8. From there all you need to do is measure your results and make adjustments based on customer behavior and feedback.

All you need to remember is: Create – Measure – Learn.

□ □ □

24. Track

I want to reiterate the importance of constant testing and analysis with everything you do in mobile. Both are essential for developing and maintaining an effective marketing strategy that delivers a positive ROI. Information is power and actionable metrics provide you with the information that matters.

Experiment and remember lifetime value of a customer (LVC) far outweighs the cost of customer acquisition when done correctly. That residual value of a customer or audience member can be measured not only in how much money they spend over time, but also by how their influence drives other sales. Can someone never purchase anything from you and still have value? Yes! They can influence others to take action. Someone who has experience with your company's product or service has much more influence when speaking about it, but their knowledge of your brand and the reputation you have will also lead to positive social interactions and potentially more sales. Don't be short sighted. See the bigger picture and learn how to shape your own future.

There is always a measurement beyond dollars and cents. Much of this goes back to customer flow and being able to identify the types of conversions that are valuable to a business. It's obvious that sales are valuable, but what about Facebook likes, Twitter followers, email and mobile subscribers? The people you engage and delight move closer to your brand as they give you permission to continue to reach out to them. This is where your analytics and metrics come into play. Alloying you to learn based on what your customers are telling you and most importantly by their behavior. Track your mobile campaigns and study how minor changes such as day, time, length of message, CTA, landing page layout, colors, pictures vs. video, and mobile channel perform differently for your audience. Over time the small changes you make to each campaign can lead to tremendous results for your business.

> **There is always a measurement
> beyond dollars and cents**

□ □ □

25. Take Action Today

I hope that you're excited about many of the opportunities in mobile marketing. No matter what your business, there are countless simple and creative ways to engage your customers. The fun comes in finding the tactics and creating content that resonates for your customers and brand. Don't be afraid to have fun with it. Mobile lends itself to experimentation. Finding the right mix can yield measurable returns, quickly.

Digital media changes rapidly. As new technology develops, I hope that you'll embrace it and find new ways to delight and serve your customers. As a culture, we are adopting the mobile lifestyle and I can only imagine that we will continue to do so. We'll spend less and less time tied to our desks, and more often we'll choose to connect while we're out in the world. As executives, marketers, business owners, startups, and thought leaders, it's imperative that we continue to evolve and to deliver consistent, useful, and relevant opportunities for engagement.

Start today!

CPSIA information can be obtained at www.ICGtesting.com
Printed in the USA
LVOW07s1819301214

420938LV00007B/1035/P

9 781499 562217